Ending
Domestic
Violence

Ending Domestic Violence

Changing Public Perceptions/Halting the Epidemic

Ethel Klein
Jacquelyn Campbell
Esta Soler
Marissa Ghez

SAGE Publications
International Educational and Professional Publisher
Thousand Oaks   London   New Delhi

For information:

SAGE Publications, Inc.
2455 Teller Road
Thousand Oaks, California 91320
E-mail: order@sagepub.com

SAGE Publications Ltd.
6 Bonhill Street
London EC2A 4PU
United Kingdom

SAGE Publications India Pvt. Ltd.
M-32 Market
Greater Kailash I
New Delhi 110 048 India

Printed in the United States of America

Library of Congress Cataloging-in-Publication Data

Ending domestic violence: changing public perceptions/halting the
epidemic / authors, Ethel Klein ... [et al.].
p. cm.
Includes bibliographical references (p.) and index.
ISBN 0-8039-7042-0 (cloth: acid-free paper). — ISBN
0-8039-7043-9 (pbk.: acid-free paper)
1. Wife abuse—United States—Public opinion. 2. Wife abuse—
United States—Prevention. 3. Family violence—United States—
Public opinion. 4. Family violence—United States—Prevention.
5. Women—Abuse of—United States. 6. Minority women—Abuse of—
United States. I. Klein, Ethel, 1952-
HV6626.2.E53 1997
362.82'927'0973—dc21   97-4801

This book is printed on acid-free paper.

97 98 99 00 01 02 03 10 9 8 7 6 5 4 3 2 1

Acquiring Editor:	C. Terry Hendrix
Editorial Assistant:	Dale Mary Grenfell
Production Editor:	Sherrise M. Purdum
Production Assistant:	Denise Santoyo
Typesetter/Designer:	Danielle Dillahunt
Indexer:	Edwin Durbin

Contents

Acknowledgments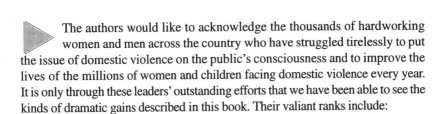

The authors would like to acknowledge the thousands of hardworking women and men across the country who have struggled tirelessly to put the issue of domestic violence on the public's consciousness and to improve the lives of the millions of women and children facing domestic violence every year. It is only through these leaders' outstanding efforts that we have been able to see the kinds of dramatic gains described in this book. Their valiant ranks include:

Karen Artichoker
David Adams
Angela Browne
Sarah Buel
Kathleen Carlin
Vickii Coffey
R. Emerson Dobash
Russell Dobash
Jeffrey Edleson
Donna Edwards
Suzanne Pharr
Donna Ferrato
Anne Flitcraft
Marie Fortune
Catlin Fullwood
Anne Ganley
Donna Garske

Ed Gondolf
Barbara Hart
Eileen Hudon
Ann Jones
Susan Kelly-Dreiss
Kerry Lobel
Del Martin
Anne Menard
Ellen Pence
Pat Reuss
Beth Richie
Susan Schechter
Hamish Sinclair
Ruth Slaughter
Evan Stark
Debby Tucker
Oliver Williams

The authors would also like to gratefully acknowledge the following individuals for their valuable assistance in completing this book:

Cathy Barenski   Julie MacPhee
Joanne Howes   Rose Smith
Darrell Kundargi   Jo Ellen Stinchcomb
Lisa Lederer

Introduction

Violence against women by their intimate partners is at least as old as recorded history and constitutes the most prevalent form of violence (in terms of proportions of people victimized) around the world (World Bank Report, 1993). It affects more women in the United States than any other form of violence and is responsible for significant mortality, injury, and threats to women's physical and mental health (Bachman & Saltzman, 1995). A cornerstone of the public health approach to any health problem is primary prevention, or preventing the problem from occurring at all. Public education and opinion are the keys to primary prevention, and media campaigns are increasingly used to inform and shape public opinion on health-related issues. Yet there have been surprisingly few scientific surveys of public knowledge and attitudes about domestic violence upon which to base primary prevention media education efforts. *Ending Domestic Violence* addresses that gap.

Public Perception Survey

This book is based on public opinion data gathered for the Family Violence Prevention Fund in 1992, prior to the development of a national public education campaign aimed at reducing the incidence of violence against women and promoting women's right to safety in the home, as well as subsequent research conducted in 1994-1996 to evaluate the efficacy and impact of that effort. The Advertising Council sponsored the campaign, bearing half the cost of the research.

In formulating the campaign, our hypothesis was that violence could be reduced by changing the attitudes of the American public about violence against women and by increasing societal involvement in the problem. The effectiveness of any primary prevention campaign depends in part on the accuracy of its perception of the attitudes it is trying to change. To plan the campaign, it was necessary to gather data about the popular understanding of domestic violence and its associated images and language.

The national public education campaign that resulted from this strategic research, called *There's No Excuse for Domestic Violence,* was launched in July 1994. The public service announcements (PSAs) produced as a part of this effort reflect research findings on how best to shape public opinion about—and ultimately, public behavior on—domestic violence. The research also adds to our general knowledge about domestic violence in the United States—including detailed information about who has been affected by the problem, who has taken some action to end the epidemic, and what some of the barriers to involvement are.

Scientists from all disciplines agree that the public context is an important determinant of the occurrence, nature, and targets of violence, although they disagree about its degree of importance. Domestic violence survivors, as well as advocates, policymakers, and scientists in the field, agree that public attitudes must change in order to end violence against women in their homes.

Witnessing domestic violence strongly affects how people perceive domestic violence and their attitudes about prevention and intervention. The research described in this book addresses for the first time the impact that witnessing domestic violence has on people's tolerance of violence and informs us about how to advise people to respond when they witness an incident of domestic violence. Does intervention place *them* in danger? Does *not* intervening or turning away encourage (or at least fail to discourage) the abusive behavior? The survey results provide some answers.

Survey Methodology

The appendixes of this publication present a detailed explanation of the methodology for each of the research studies described. The following is an overview. During the first stage of the research, prior to the development of the *There's No Excuse* initiative, EDK Associates worked with the Family Violence Prevention Fund to gather data from 12 focus groups in five cities nationwide— three groups of white women, two of white men, two of African American women, one of African American men, and one each of Latino and Asian American men and Latina and Asian American women. The Latino groups were conducted in Spanish. Each group's facilitator matched the members' ethnicity;

members' education level varied. Each group comprised an average of 10 participants. All the meetings were audiotaped and transcribed. Researchers analyzed both latent and manifest content to determine first the text and presentation for use in the next stage of research—the survey. Verbatim quotes from the groups also illustrate and amplify the survey results. This set of research will be referred to henceforth as the EDK focus groups.

On the basis of information gathered through the focus groups, EDK Associates developed a national public opinion survey and conducted a national random telephone interview of 1,000 people ages 18 and over, with an equal number of males and females. To allow for demographic analysis across gender and ethnicity, we included an additional, shortened telephone interview, using the same questions, of 300 Latinos and 300 African Americans. This research shall be referred to in the text as the EDK poll or EDK survey.

Beginning in 1994, the Family Violence Prevention Fund partnered with Lieberman Research, Inc., to track public opinion about domestic violence over the course of its *There's No Excuse* campaign, in order to evaluate the efficacy of the campaign and prevailing attitudes and behavior on the issue of violence against women. In addition to a benchmark wave of polling that took place in July 1994, immediately prior to the distribution of the campaign's first round of advertising, subsequent waves of national polling were conducted in November 1994-February 1995, November 1995, and October 1996. Each wave of polling consisted of a random sample of at least 700 Computer-Assisted Telephone Interviews (CATI) with women and men 18 to 65 years of age (divided equally between genders). As this book went to press, results from the final wave of polling in October 1996 were not ready for release and therefore are not reported in this publication. The methodology for each wave of polling is reported in greater detail in Appendix C. These surveys shall be henceforth referred to as the Lieberman polls or surveys, along with the corresponding date.

Finally, we do not dispute that women both engage in abusive behavior toward men and are sometimes the primary perpetrators in abusive relationships. However, we are convinced that the most severe violence, that which causes injury, is most often directed at women by men (Bachman, 1994). Our surveys demonstrate that the public is primarily concerned with diminishing the problem of domestic violence perpetrated by men against women, and that is the focus of this publication.

Ethnicity and Class

The research presented here adds to our knowledge about the relationship of ethnicity to public perceptions and experiences of domestic violence, a subject that has been largely overlooked in the literature. Domestic violence is embedded within the framework of a patriarchal culture that permits men to beat women. To ignore culture and its intertwining relationship with race and ethnicity is to ignore an important part of the explanations and the solutions regarding domestic violence. In an effort to be sensitive to the issue of ethnicity, the research reported here included focus groups of different ethnicities led by people of that same culture. In addition, our 1992 baseline EDK poll used oversampling in the primary ethnic groups to obtain a diverse, multiethnic representation. We also sampled across educational categories among all ethnicities and used education as a control variable to avoid confounding class factors as they intersect with ethnicity.

Women's income and occupation are also problematic as indicators of "class"-related values for women. They are too often determined by marital status, age of children, and/or a husband's or partner's preferences. Women and people of color of both genders are excluded from certain occupations because of discrimination. Therefore, they are not represented in income categories that would otherwise be commensurate with their education and value systems. For these reasons, we used education as the most salient proxy across genders and ethnic groups for socioeconomic status (SES).

With respect to the Lieberman polls, although non-Anglo ethnic groups were sampled proportionate to their percentages in the general population, the failure to appropriately oversample resulted in ethnic groupings that were too small to interpret differences with confidence. Thus these additional polls provide the most recent information about the current landscape of public opinion about domestic violence, but they are not as complete as the EDK poll demographically.

To enrich our understanding of the cultural context as it relates to domestic violence, a woman of color from the three major ethnic groups represented in the research (African American, Latina, and Asian American), each an expert in domestic violence, contributed to the findings and conclusions of the study. They collaborated on Chapter 5 ("Water on Rock") and assisted us in interpreting the survey results specific to their ethnic group. The three authors are Doris Campbell, Ph.D., R.N., professor of nursing at the University of Florida and a member of the Florida Governor's Commission on Domestic Violence; Sara Torres, Ph.D., R.N., associate professor and associate dean of nursing at the University of Maryland and an expert on the cultural context (especially Latina) of violence against women; and Beckie Masaki, executive director of the Asian Women's Shelter in San Francisco, a member of the board of directors of the Family Violence Prevention Fund, and an expert on Asian American women's responses to intimate partner violence. We want to acknowledge formally the importance of their contribution.

Text Overview

Chapter 1, "Domestic Violence in Public Context," details the history of the battered women's movement, including a discussion of important changes in public concern about the problem. Chapter 2, "Violence as Part of Everyday Life," examines public perceptions of the extent of domestic violence, as well as people's own personal experience of the problem. The public attribution of blame for domestic violence is discussed in Chapter 3, "Why Does Domestic Violence Happen?" Chapter 4, "Drawing the Line," looks at the point at which the public is willing to intervene. Chapter 5, "Water on Rock," described above, focuses on ethnicity. The implications of this research for changing public opinion and behavior are explored in Chapter 6, "Public Education Campaigns on Domestic Violence." The appendixes describe the methodologies used in the research reported in this book. *Ending Domestic Violence* offers a cogent and detailed picture of how Americans perceive the issue of domestic violence at the turn of the 20th century, and how best to persuade them to get involved in putting an end to it in the 21st. The Family Violence Prevention Fund's *There's No Excuse for Domestic Violence* campaign is only a first step in that process.

Domestic Violence in Public Context

Historical Context

One of the great achievements of feminism was to define wife beating as a social problem, not merely a phenomenon of particular violent individuals or relationships. Women have historically resisted battering—physically. But in the past hundred years, they began to resist it politically and ideologically, with considerable success (Gordon, 1988).

Some recorded vestiges do exist showing examples of public protest against wife beating from Roman times and during the French Revolution (Campbell, 1991; Dobash & Dobash, 1979). However, the first well-documented political campaign against wife battering, known as the first wave of feminism, took place in Great Britain in the late 19th century (May, 1978). In contrast, the United States addressed domestic violence in the late 19th century only as a part of the temperance, child welfare, and social housekeeping movements (Gordon, 1988). Wife abuse in America was seen as disreputable but not a topic for public discussion, let alone protest.

In a contemporary review of child abuse cases in Boston, Gordon (1988) found that women whose husbands abused their children considered their *own* abuse by the husband inevitable. They tried to resist by fleeing, fighting back, calling the police or other community agents, appealing to kin, or asking for the abuser's sympathy. Throughout history, women have used these same strategies. In postrevolutionary France, divorce petitions from the city of Lyon document battered women's experiences (Campbell, 1991). Evidence of wife beating is also seen in Abigail Abbot Bailey's account from 18th century New Hampshire (Taves, 1989); Mark Mathabane's (1994) report of a grandmother's, mother's,

1

and sister's abuse in 20th-century South Africa; and numerous accounts by women from around the world who have been beaten by their male intimate partners (Counts, Brown, & Campbell, 1992). The more things change, the more they stay the same.

Yet, in the 20th century, social and political changes *have* occurred, and women of all countries are beginning to believe that they have the right to live without violence. Battered women are realizing that they are not alone; they have seen too many women like themselves on television talk shows to feel as isolated as their counterparts did as recently as 20 years ago. Since that time, wife beating has become a common topic for public debate, if not public censure, in most countries. This monumental shift in both public and private perception is the result of the sustained effort by the grassroots battered women's movement over the past two decades.

History of the Battered Women's Movement

The battered women's movement began with the second wave of feminism in the United States in the early 1970s. Its strength and success drew on the previous social influences of the antiwar and civil rights campaigns of the 1960s. Battered women's efforts also stemmed from earlier protests against sexual assault that were some of the first expressions of feminist activism decrying violence toward women. As Susan Schechter (1982) pointed out, 1970s feminism created both a climate for women to speak out about violence and a structure through which they could organize.

Shelters for abused women arose in every major community in the United States during the 1970s and 1980s. Often founded by coalitions of formerly battered women, feminist activists (some closely aligned with organizations such as the National Organization for Women [NOW]), and veterans of rape crisis centers, the shelters are a wonderful example of the ability of grassroots organizations to render services for individual women and for social change. From their inception, shelters have tried to provide public education and training for professionals in the criminal justice system and to offer leadership in legal reform as well as shelter, safety, and advocacy for battered women and their children.

Research and the Battered Women's Movement

The "science" was right in step with the activism at first. The early books on wife abuse were models of scholarly products written for the public. Rebecca and Russell Dobash (1979) used a combination of historical research and interviews with battered women to substantiate their theoretical framework regarding patriarchy as the basic causative factor in wife beating. Dell Martin's

(1976) groundbreaking work first alerted the American public and scientific community to the realities of wife abuse. This research effectively refuted prior studies of wife abuse, specifically psychiatric case studies from the 1960s that emphasized the women's "masochistic tendencies" (e.g., Snell, Rosenwald, & Robey, 1964).

However, the statistical analysis, the sampling, and the measurement used in the early research were unsophisticated. The problem had become legitimized and some funding was available for further research, which attracted new scholars to the field. This new wave of researchers was not necessarily made up of activists or feminists. In general, these researchers conceptualized wife abuse as a form of "family violence" rather than as violence against women. They were primarily sociologists who relied heavily on interactive, family systems, and/or social learning theories of domestic violence causation (e.g., Straus, Gelles, & Steinmetz, 1980). For these sociologists, the abuse of intimate partners was originally seen as the extreme end of family *conflict,* and therefore an example of a family systems process, rather than as an instance of violence against women and a manifestation of the oppression of women.

This fundamental conceptual difference shaped the findings of the research, which was otherwise a model of telephone survey research. The sociological research on wife abuse provided the first national random survey (therefore scientifically persuasive) estimates of the prevalence of wife abuse as well as child abuse. These results legitimized national concern about the problem and were widely publicized.

Also publicized were data from the same surveys showing that women used abusive tactics in marital disagreements as often as men did. There has been no perfect and definitive survey research to date in the United States on the prevalence and incidence of domestic violence, and the gender controversy in terms of statistics as well as cause has continued to be a polarizing issue between the battered women's movement and some members of the research community. The conflict is often exploited in the popular press, to the detriment of scholars and laypersons alike.

International Context

Battered women's movements developed in Canada and Western Europe during the same time period. Great Britain had led the way with the creation of the first wife abuse shelter in 1970. However, less industrialized countries are only just beginning to recognize the problem publicly and establish services. Worldwide statistics show that wife beating occurs in 84% of small-scale societies (Levinson, 1989) and 100% of more "developed" societies. When women in less industrialized countries were polled, they listed violence as the health problem of greatest concern to them (Heise, Pitanguy, & Germain, 1994). Yet wife beating was not officially considered under the purview of international action; rather, the emic view (from within the culture) was taken. The United Nations finally included violence against women as a human rights violation at its International Conference on Human Rights, which took place in Vienna in 1993. That same year, the World Bank (1993) also recognized wife beating as a significant economic problem in terms of health costs. These official actions signaled inclusion in the public international domain (versus cultural normative and therefore private) and paved the way for increased official global efforts at prevention, alleviation, and incorporation in developmental and health programs (Desjarlais, Eisenberg, Good, & Kleiman, 1995).

Sanctions Against Battering

Public sanctions against wife beating have been crucial to the field of domestic violence. In their cultural analysis of primary data from anthropologists about 14 distinct cultures worldwide, Counts et al. (1992) concluded that sanctions against abuse and sanctuary for beaten women were the most important factors in preventing occasional wife beating from escalating to more ongoing wife battering. Effective sanctions were applied by the community or neighborhood, rather than only national proclamations or laws, but such national attention often preceded local action.

In their study, Counts and her colleagues (1992) used primary ethnographic evidence collected from 14 different societies representing a range of geographic locations, level of industrialization, type of household arrangements, and degree of spousal violence. They examined evidence supporting the primary theoretical stances about battering from Western social sciences. Although the feminist (or patriarchal) theoretical premises received considerable support, several aspects were brought into question. The review suggested that all forms of violence against women could not be considered as aspects of the same phenomenon and that the status of women is an extremely complex, multifaceted phenomenon that may have a curvilinear rather than direct relationship with wife battering. In other words, women who are kept totally controlled by societal norms may not "need" to be beaten by individual male partners. At the lower end of the curve, where there is true gender equality across all the aspects of status and power, there would also be relatively little wife beating. At the center of the curve, where male and female gender roles and relative power are in flux and in contention, the most wife beating would occur. Although this proposition has not been tested, it is supported by other analyses (e.g., Levinson, 1989).

The Counts et al. (1992) review also demonstrated the importance of other societal influences on individual couples. Wife beating (defined as occasional and nonescalating, without serious or permanent injury, seen as ordinary by most members of the culture, and occurring in almost all societies in the world) was differentiated from wife battering. Battering was defined as the continuing, usually escalating, potentially injurious pattern of physical violence within a context of coercive control most often described in Western social sciences and health research. Community-level sanctions against battering and sanctuary for beaten wives, enacted in culturally specific and appropriate forms, were found to discourage the escalation of wife beating to battering across societies (Counts et al., 1992).

Community-Level Sanctions: Examples

Many small communities have practices that seek to prevent a small minority of men who have occasionally hit their wives from escalating to the kind of widespread chronic and serious battering that is common in the United States. From Africa to South and Central America to the Pacific Islands, there are community-level cultural practices that could be modified and emulated in our communities (examples from Counts et al., 1992).

For instance, on the Muslim island of Mayotte off the eastern coast of Africa, male wife abusers are sent home to their own kin to learn better domestic behavior. Among the Nagovisi people of the Solomon Islands of Oceania, kin and community courts immediately intervene at the first sign of domestic violence. Ecuadorian villagers recognize the potential for domestic violence in young couples, especially with a cultural norm of *machismo,* and assign all newlyweds a *compadre* who is responsible for guarding against wife abuse and intervening at the first sign of discord. In another community where there is a cultural norm of machismo, the Marshall Islanders of Oceania use community chastisement of abusive men. The village elders are quickly brought in when a couple shows signs of conflict.

In New Guinea, where many cultural groups condone severe levels of wife battering, the Wape are an exception. If someone hears loud shouting between a couple, the women of the Wape village surround the identified house and stand around it until the woman joins them outside. The Garifuna people of Belize, in Central America, are another example of female community solidarity. The Garifuna are descended from Africans and indigenous Caribbean Indians, with primarily African appearance and cultural norms but without a history of slavery. In Garifuna villages, the climate is warm and people's houses have open windows. Villagers spend much of life outdoors, and kin and other women respond when they hear sounds of a fight developing between members of a couple. They come to the scene and stand by as witnesses, providing at the least a shaming function and, if the abuse is very serious, interfering directly. Among the !Kung of Africa, neighbors will help, and relatives will rescue beaten women if needed.

These are community-action models: of neighbor helping neighbor, women alerting other women, kin intervening, and community leaders seeing domestic violence as a threat to the collective order and taking action accordingly. These actions could also be taken in small rural and suburban communities and on the urban neighborhood level. They could be incorporated into existing neighborhood watches, in church groups, and in Head Start and school parent groups, family reunions, union groups, and the like.

Unlike the situation in societies where battering has been minimized, the majority of a sample of batterers in the United States perceived *no* public sanctions against them for abusing their wives, according to Carmody and Williams (1987). The batterers had neither experienced nor did they expect any serious negative consequences—legal, occupational, or social. The expectation of negative repercussions is rarely sufficient to change behavior in and of itself, but it can sometimes influence a batterer. Although rational, cognitive decision making is not commonly attributed to batterers, most domestic batterers do, in effect, choose *not* to hit their bosses or police officers, no matter how angry or "out of control" they are.

In the United States, wife abuse has traditionally been seen as a private matter. But public perceptions are changing, just as they are in other areas of public health concern. Public education initiatives can have a tremendous impact in changing behavior, particularly in arenas where individuals need to be given permission and encouragement to challenge other people's actions that were once thought to be "none of their business."

For example, Mothers Against Drunk Driving (MADD) has influenced public opinion about alcohol use and has encouraged the public to take both individual responsibility and collective action. Not that long ago, people would have felt uncomfortable demanding that someone else give up their car keys if they had drunk too much, or asking someone not to smoke. Today, based on findings of the EDK poll, we can say that almost all Americans (95%) claim they would ask a friend who had too much to drink at a party for the car keys and insist on driving the friend home. And if they were sitting in a nonsmoking section in a restaurant and someone was smoking, many respondents (57%) said they would ask that person (or ask the waiter to ask the person) to stop smoking (see Table 1.1).

There is increasing recognition in the field of public health that social environmental factors are as important as individual motivation and support for making behavioral change. The social environment includes neighbors, friends, coworkers, and even acquaintances who take responsibility for monitoring and/or attempting to change the behaviors of others for the good of the whole "community." This has been part of the message of the MADD campaign, that all citizens must take individual and collective action regarding social and public health issues, even if they are not directly involved in the problem. Personal accountability

TABLE 1.1 Vignettes: Social Support for Intervention

	Percentage of Respondents Saying Yes		
	All	*Women*	*Men*
If you were sitting in a nonsmoking section in a restaurant and someone was smoking, would you ask that person or get the waiter to ask that person to stop smoking?	57	57	57
If you were at a party and a friend of yours had too much to drink, would you ask him or her for the car keys and insist on driving your friend home?	95	95	96
If a friend of yours complained about his wife screaming and hitting on him to the point where he said he had to slap her to calm her down, would you tell him that he should have walked away rather than hit her?	83	84	83

SOURCE: These data are from a 1992 poll conducted by EDK Associates, working with the Family Violence Prevention Fund. For details see Appendix B.

comes from believing that the problem is widespread and of sufficient threat to the community fabric that it affects one's own life—enough to take action. The public must also perceive that the problem is amenable to intervention.

A similar, concerted public education effort targeting domestic violence could increase the number of Americans who would no longer implicitly sanction violence toward women by remaining silent. By encouraging people to feel a sense of permission to challenge battering, we hope to see more widespread behavioral change.

Saliency: Does Domestic Violence Touch Our Lives?

As with any other issue, the ability to increase public involvement in efforts to reduce domestic violence is partially shaped by how salient this problem is perceived to be to people's personal lives. Men and women today worry about a host of social concerns, including crime and drugs, pollution and environmental problems, health care, day care, and AIDS, as well as the problem of family violence. Placing personal levels of concern about family violence within this constellation reveals how important this issue ranks on people's agenda and how it compares to other important social issues (see Table 1.2).

In 1992, as we developed our campaign, respondents to the EDK poll said they were most worried about AIDS (53%). The second-tier issues about which they were very concerned included health care (43%) and crime and drugs

TABLE 1.2 Putting Concern About Domestic Violence in the Context of Other
            Social Issues

The Social Agenda	*Percentage Responding* Very Worried/Extremely Important		
	All *(N = 1,008)*	*Women* *(n = 505)*	*Men* *(n = 503)*
AIDS	53	57	49
Health care[a]	43	46	39
Crime and drugs[a]	42	52	33
Pollution	37	41	32
Domestic violence[a]	34	43	25
Day care	12	15	9

SOURCE: These data are from a 1992 poll conducted by EDK Associates, working with the Family
Violence Prevention Fund. For details see Appendix B.

a. Gender differences significant at $p < .05$.

(42%). Personal concern for family violence (34%) joined pollution (37%) as
the next level of salient social issues. Day care was very low on the list; barely
1 out of 10 respondents saw this as a personal worry (12%).

    Since 1992, there has been a tremendous change in the way people think
about and relate to the issue of domestic violence. Prompted in part by the trial
of O. J. Simpson for the murder of his ex-wife and the subsequent revelations
of his battery of her for many years, a national "teach-in" on the issue of domestic
violence occurred in the summer of 1994, generated by hundreds of articles and
stories about the issue in media outlets around the country. The media focus on
domestic violence did not go unnoticed by the general public—in July 1994, an
astounding 78% of respondents to the Lieberman survey reported that they had
seen stories about domestic violence in the media in the previous 3 months, and
the number remained quite high (67%) more than a year later, in the November
1995 Lieberman poll (see Table 1.3).

    What's more, almost three in four respondents (72%) to the Lieberman poll
in November 1995 reported having learned something about domestic violence
from the media coverage of the O. J. Simpson trial (see Table 1.4). Most strikingly,
most respondents said they had learned that domestic violence is a serious
problem (93%) and that the family and friends of abused women need to learn
more about how to help victims of domestic violence (91%) (see Table 1.5).

    As a result, Americans now rank domestic violence as an extremely important
problem and perceive the problem as more salient. The question was asked
slightly differently in the Lieberman surveys than in the previous EDK polls (for
example, AIDS was not included as a concern and a different stem was used).
But in the November 1995 Lieberman poll, the most recent one for which results

TABLE 1.3 Percentage of Respondents Who Saw Domestic Violence Stories in the
Media in the Previous 3 Months: Changes Over Time

	July 1994 (N = 735)	January-February 1995[a] (N = 486)	November 1995 (N = 742)	January-February 1995 Versus November 1995
Very often	49	45	39	-6^{b}
Fairly often	29	27	28	+1
Not too often	14	21	23	+2
Not at all often	7	7	9	+2
Don't remember	1	—	1	+1

SOURCE: These data are from polls conducted by Lieberman Research, Inc., working with the Family
Violence Prevention Fund and The Advertising Council. For details see Appendix C.

a. The second wave of polling by Lieberman Research took place from November 1994 to February 1995.
However, data from the shorter January-February period were used here so that they would be more
comparable to the first- and third-wave polls, which were conducted in a single month.

b. Significantly lower with a 95% confidence interval.

are available, domestic violence was ranked *first* in importance, slightly (but not
significantly) more important than street crime or children living in poverty.
Concerns about the environment, teenage alcoholism, and teenage pregnancy
were lower on the list (see Table 1.6).

Who Cares About Domestic Violence?

As the landscape of public perception continues to change around the issue
of domestic violence, so, too, does the composition of the constituency of people
who care most about the issue. Important changes have occurred in the past
several years regarding *who* appears to be concerned about the issue of domestic
violence. As public mobilization efforts are best aimed at those who care most
about a particular issue, researchers and advocates seeking to craft effective
awareness and activation messages on the issue of violence against women must
assess these shifts carefully.

In 1992, the EDK poll indicates, women tended to be more personally
concerned than men about social issues. These differences were greatest on
issues of violence in general, as in crime and drugs and, most strikingly and more
specifically, violence in the family. One in two (52%) women compared to one
in three (33%) men said they were personally very worried about crime and
drugs. Four in ten women (43%)—compared to one in four men (25%)—were
very worried about the growth of family violence. In fact, a sizable percentage

TABLE 1.4 Amount Learned About Domestic Violence From Media Coverage of
O. J. Simpson Trial

Percentage of Respondents Who:	Total U.S. (N = 742)	California (n = 202)
Learned something[a]	72	76
Learned a lot	22	31
Learned a fair amount	26	27
Learned a little	24	18
Learned nothing at all	27	24
Not aware of the trial	1	

SOURCE: These data are from a November 1995 poll conducted by Lieberman Research, Inc., working with the Family Violence Prevention Fund and The Advertising Council. For details see Appendix C.
a. This is the total of those who said they learned a lot/a fair amount/a little.

of men said that they did not worry about this problem at all (29% compared to 11% of women).

Race and ethnicity interacted with gender in shaping the personal saliency of family violence, according to the EDK poll. There were significant gender differences in the level of concern among Caucasians (42% of women were very worried compared to 22% of men) and Latinos (43% vs. 35%) but not among African Americans (40% vs. 37%) or Asian Americans (19% vs. 26%). Caucasian women rated this issue as most worrisome (42%), whereas Caucasian and Asian American men saw the issue as personally least troubling. Nearly one out of three Caucasian (32%) and Asian American (30%) men said they were not worried by the growth of family violence (see Table 1.7).

Concern for the growth of family violence was a function of income and education for Caucasian women but not for any other group in the EDK poll. The percentage of women very worried about the growth of family violence decreased from 49% among Caucasian women with household incomes of under $25,000, to 33% among households earning $25,000 to $44,000, to 26% for those with incomes of $45,000 or more. There was a curvilinear relationship with education. Concern was higher among women with a high school diploma or less (42%) than among those with some college (36%). The percentage concerned increased for those with college degrees (42%) and postgraduate education (50%). According to the National Victim Survey (Bachman, 1994), the "some college" education group was the group that was *most* likely to experience serious assault from an intimate partner. Age and marital status had no influence on how worried any group was about the issue of growth in family violence.

By late 1995, following the massive national media coverage on the issue, the landscape had changed considerably (see Table 1.8). Data collected by

TABLE 1.5 Agreement With Statements About Information Learned From Media
Coverage of O. J. Simpson Trial

	Percentage of Respondents Who:	
I Learned That:	*Agree Strongly/ Somewhat (n = 513)*	*Disagree Strongly/ Somewhat (n = 513)*
Domestic violence is a serious problem	93	5
The family and friends of abused women need to learn more about how to help victims of domestic violence	91	8
Physically abusive men are not always arrested by the police or prosecuted in court	89	9
Police and judges need to learn more about domestic violence and how to handle domestic violence situations	88	8
Women who are physically abused by their husbands or boyfriends are more likely than other women to be killed by them	86	12
Domestic violence is wrong, but it is usually just about two people arguing	34	64

SOURCE: These data are from a November 1995 poll conducted by Lieberman Research, Inc., working with the Family Violence Prevention Fund and The Advertising Council. For details see Appendix C.

NOTE: Only those respondents who said they had heard these statements were asked whether and how strongly they agreed with them.

Lieberman Research throughout 1994 and 1995 reveal substantial shifts in the perceived importance of domestic violence among various demographic groups. Perhaps the most striking of these shifts occurred among men in the United States, who in the span of one short year began to see the issue of domestic violence as significantly more important than they had before—in the Lieberman poll conducted from November 1994 to February 1995, only 25% of men respondents considered domestic violence an extremely important problem, whereas in the November 1995 Lieberman survey, 33% did so. This is a remarkable shift considering that in the same time period, the percentage of women respondents who considered domestic violence a serious problem, although higher than that of men, remained static at 44%.

The Lieberman polls record other important shifts in this time period. By November 1995, city dwellers across the United States were significantly more concerned about domestic violence than their counterparts in the suburbs (48% of city dwellers vs. 27% of suburbanites identified domestic violence as an extremely important problem). And even in geographic areas where concern was

TABLE 1.6 Changes in the Levels of Concern About Domestic Violence, Other
Social Issues

	Percentage Responding Extremely/Very Important			
Social Issues	July 1994 (N = 735)	January-February 1995[a] (N = 486)	November 1995 (N = 742)	January-February 1995 Versus November 1995
Domestic violence	79	80	83	+3
Street crime	84	87	81	−6[b]
Children living in poverty	81	83	82	−1
The environment	77	77	74	−3
Teenage alcoholism	71	70	71	+1
Teenage pregnancy	68	70	69	−1

SOURCE: These data are from polls conducted by Lieberman Research, Inc., working with the Family
Violence Prevention Fund and The Advertising Council. For details see Appendix C.

a. The second wave of polling by Lieberman Research took place from November 1994 to February 1995.
However, data from the shorter January-February period were used here so that they would be more
comparable to the first- and third-wave polls, which were conducted in a single month.

b. Significantly lower with a 95% confidence interval.

relatively high by November 1995, that level of concern was relatively new:
Although 48% of city dwellers considered domestic violence an extremely
important problem in November 1995, only 37% identified it as such in the
Lieberman polls that occurred only a year earlier.

Similarly, there were dramatic shifts in the percentage of people ages 50 to
65 who identified domestic violence as a serious concern to them. Whereas in
the November 1995 Lieberman poll, 42% of 50- to 65-year-old respondents

TABLE 1.7 Percentage of Respondents Worried About the Growth of Family
Violence, by Ethnicity and Gender

	Caucasians		African Americans		Latinos/Latinas		Asian Americans	
	Women (n = 395)	Men (n = 308)	Women (n = 218)	Men (n = 188)	Women (n = 156)	Men (n = 161)	Women (n = 156)	Men (n = 161)
Very worried	43[a]	23	41	37	44[a]	35	20	26
Worried	46	45	37	37	45	42	50	45
Not worried	11[a]	33	22	26	11[a]	22	30	28

SOURCE: These data are from a 1992 poll conducted by EDK Associates, working with the Family
Violence Prevention Fund. For details see Appendix B.

a. Gender differences within racial/ethnic group are significant at $p < .05$.

TABLE 1.8 Importance of Domestic Violence Among Different Demographic Groups

| | Percentage Responding: | | | | | | | | |
| | Extremely Important | | | | Extremely/Very Important | | | | |
	July 1994	November 1994-February 1995	November 1995	February 1995 Versus November 1995	July 1994	November 1994-February 1995	November 1995	February 1995 Versus November 1995	November 1995 (Average Base)
Total	35	35	38	+3	79	79	83	+4[a]	(820)
California	36	40	39	−1	88	80	87	+7[a]	(229)
Gender									
Female	42	44	44	0	84	86	86	±0	(412)
Male	27	25	33	+8[a]	74	73	79	+6[a]	(408)
Age									
18 to 34 years	39	36	40	+4	82	80	83	+3	(333)
35 to 49 years	31	35	35	±0	75	80	81	+1	(303)
50 to 65 years	31	31	42	+11[a]	79	76	84	+8	(176)
Household income									
Under $20,000	49	40	49	+9	88	85	83	−2	(161)
$20,000 to $39,999	31	35	34	−1	81	80	81	+1	(239)
$40,000 or more	26	32	29	−3	72	76	79	+3	(303)
Type of area									
City	42	37	48	+11[a]	85	81	90	+9[a]	(210)
Suburban	29	32	27	−5	76	74	78	+4	(278)
Small town/rural	34	35	41	+6	78	83	82	−1	(329)

SOURCE: These data are from polls conducted by Lieberman Research, Inc., working with the Family Violence Prevention Fund and The Advertising Council. For details see Appendix C.
a. Significantly higher with a 95% confidence interval.

considered domestic violence an extremely important problem, only 31% did
so in the poll conducted a year earlier. Similar gains were not reflected in other
age categories.

In some important areas, less change was noticeable. As in the earlier EDK
polls, the November 1995 Lieberman poll showed that lower-income individuals remained more concerned about domestic violence than either middle- or
upper-income respondents. About 49% of individuals from households earning
less than $20,000 income identified domestic violence as an extremely impor-
tant problem, compared to 34% of individuals from households earning $20,000
to $39,999 and 29% of individuals from households earning $40,000 or more.

Does Personal Exposure Increase Saliency?

In 1992, as we began our thinking about who was most likely to care about
the issue of domestic violence, we speculated that exposure to domestic violence
probably increased the personal saliency of the issue of battering. EDK polling
results proved this to be marginally true for women but not for men (see Table
1.9). Women who had witnessed a loud, threatening confrontation between a
couple were more likely to say that they were very worried about the growth in
family violence than women who had not (49% vs. 38%). Yet witnessing such
a confrontation did not increase the saliency of family violence among men
(23% vs. 28%).

Overall, women in the EDK poll worried about the escalation of family
violence independent of whether they had personally witnessed battering. Those
who reported having observed a man beating a woman were only slightly more
worried about family violence than those who had not (46% vs. 42%). This
suggests that the threat of violence is pervasive enough that women who have
not witnessed it still worry about it.

On the other hand, men in the EDK poll were not concerned about the escalation
of family violence even when they reported having witnessed a man beating his
wife or girlfriend. Only one in four men were very worried about the growth in
family violence, whether they had witnessed battering (26%) or not (24%). Three
out of ten men who had witnessed male violence toward a wife or girlfriend said
that the growth in family violence was not an important issue to them.

By 1995, however, both women and men appear to have reached a threshold
of concern about domestic violence that seems independent of their personal
connection to individuals who have faced abuse, perhaps due to the extensive
media coverage the issue had recently received. This finding of the Lieberman
surveys is particularly dramatic for women: Between July 1994 and November
1995, the percentage of women respondents who said they knew a victim of
domestic violence jumped significantly from 32% to 42%—yet in that same
time period, the percentage of women respondents who identified domestic

TABLE 1.9 Exposure to Family Violence Related to Concern Expressed in Survey

	Women		Men	
	Yes	*No*	*Yes*	*No*
Have you ever witnessed people yelling loudly at one another and threatening to get violent?[a]				
Very worried about family violence	49	38	23	28
Worried	43	45	45	44
Not worried	7	14	31	27
Have you ever witnessed a person beating a child?[b]				
Very worried about family violence	54	41	32	22
Worried	36	46	38	47
Not worried	9	11	30	29
Have you ever witnessed a man beating his wife or girlfriend?[c]				
Very worried about family violence	46	42	26	24
Worried	42	45	44	45
Not worried	11	10	29	29

SOURCE: These data are from a 1992 poll conducted by EDK Associates, working with the Family Violence Prevention Fund. For details see Appendix B.

NOTE: This table shows how exposure to family violence—as expressed by the answers to the questions in the table—was related to respondents' level of concern about such violence, as measured by a separate survey question. Numbers are the percentage of those answering yes or no to the question who said they were *very worried, worried,* or *not worried* about family violence.

a. These differences in response were significant for women at $p < .01$ and nonsignificant for men.

b. These differences in response were significant for women at $p < .09$ and nonsignificant for men.

c. These differences in response were nonsignificant for men and women.

violence as an extremely important problem remained relatively static (42% in July 1994 vs. 44% in November 1995) (see Table 1.10).

As in the earlier EDK poll, the Lieberman surveys found that men's perception about the seriousness of the problem seems independent of their knowledge of individual victims of abuse. Although there was a significant jump in the percentage of men who considered domestic violence an extremely important problem between July 1994 (27%) and November 1995 (33%), the proportion of men respondents who said they knew victims of domestic violence remained relatively the same over that time period (26% vs. 28%).

Interestingly, in the November 1995 Lieberman poll, respondents from middle-income households ($20,000 to $39,999) were most likely to say they *knew* an abused woman (46%, compared with 34% from households earning less than $20,000 and 31% from households earning more than $40,000). Yet those who were most likely to identify domestic violence as a serious problem were those coming from lower-income households (49%, as compared with 34% of individuals from middle-income households and 29% from lower-income households).

TABLE 1.10 Percentage of Respondents Who Know Women Who Are Physically Abused, by Demographic Group: Changes Over Time

	July 1994	November 1994-February 1995	November 1995	November 1994-February 1995 Versus November 1995	(Average Base)
Total	29	33	35	+2	(820)
California	32	38	37	−1	(229)
Gender					
Female	32	40	42	+2	(412)
Male	26	25	28	+3	(408)
Age					
18 to 34 years	35	32	41	+9[a]	(333)
35 to 49 years	30	35	33	−2	(303)
50 to 65 years	17	28	24	−4	(176)
Household income					
Under $20,000	33	40	34	−6	(161)
$20,000 to $39,999	32	28	46	+18[a]	(239)
$40,000 or more	25	35	31	−4	(303)
Type of area					
City	37	28	42	+14[a]	(210)
Suburban	30	32	33	+1	(278)
Small town/rural	24	36	33	−3	(329)

SOURCE: These data are from polls conducted by Lieberman Research, Inc., working with the Family Violence Prevention Fund and The Advertising Council. For details see Appendix C.

a. Significantly higher with a 95% confidence interval.

Summary

Major gains in the battered women's movement have occurred in the past 25 years. Shelters to help women and children facing violence at home have sprung up in communities all over the country, and social and political advances have been made in both the domestic and international arenas. In more recent years, the American public has learned a tremendous amount about the severity and impact of domestic violence, as well as its relevancy to their lives. These steps have been major, and our surveys show they have forever changed the way that Americans perceive the problem of domestic violence, as well as their relationship to it. Drawing on the successes of other social change movements, we can capitalize on the high level of concern about the problem that exists today by creating public education campaigns that transform the culture of acceptance that has existed for centuries around the issue of violence against women.

Violence as a Part of Everyday Life

Our personal lives are not immune to violence inflicted by the people we love. Even before the extensive media coverage about domestic violence generated in recent years and the important legislative changes that have occurred, including the passage of the landmark Violence Against Women Act in 1994, Americans acknowledged a pervasive amount of violence in private relationships. Yet the issue had for so long been shrouded in silence that at the outset of our work, getting people to talk about domestic violence was considered a major obstacle to conducting both the focus groups and survey research. Experts believed that people would refuse to open up in the groups or to stay on the phone once they understood the topic.

The experts were wrong. One of the most striking findings of this research is that Americans of all racial and ethnic backgrounds are both ready and willing to discuss this issue. People in the focus groups and on the phone discussed domestic violence as a real problem that they have seen in their own lives. And they want it to end.

We Hurt the Ones We Love

In the 1992 EDK poll, shoving and pushing and throwing objects were not considered rare occurrences when a man and a woman have a fight. This survey showed that the public was not willing to draw a line that puts women on the good side and men on the bad. But, as the severity of physical violence increases, both men and women acknowledged that men harm women more than women harm men.

TABLE 2.1 Percentage of Respondents Who Said They Had Witnessed Various
Acts of Violence in Private Relationships

	Male Perpetrator			Female Perpetrator		
	All	Women	Men	All	Women	Men
Says nasty things						
Often	48	52[a]	45	44	52[a]	54
Sometimes	33	30	36	34	32	37
Rarely	11	9	13	19	11	15
Don't know	8	9	8	9	9	9
Grabs and shoves her						
Often	24	28[a]	20	11	13[b]	9
Sometimes	33	33	32	29	29	28
Rarely	30	25	32	48	45	51
Don't know	13	13	12	12	12	12
Throws something						
Often	13	16[a]	9	26	29[a]	24
Sometimes	28	27	24	29	31	27
Rarely	49	41	56	34	28	39
Don't know	13	15	11	11	12	10
Beats badly						
Often	19	23[a]	15	5	6	4
Sometimes	25	29	22	11	11	10
Rarely	43	35	51	72	69	75
Don't know	13	14	11	13	14	11

SOURCE: These data are from a 1992 poll conducted by EDK Associates, working with the Family
Violence Prevention Fund. For details see Appendix B.
a. Differences are significant at $p = .00$.
b. Differences are significant at $p = .04$.

One in two women in the EDK survey said they believe that battering is not
an uncommon experience in women's relationships with men (see Table 2.1).
Some 44% of respondents said they believe that when a man and a woman fight,
he could wind up hitting her. Some people believed this happened often (19%),
but more likely only sometimes (25%). Less than half said it rarely happens
(43%). Men were significantly more likely than women to see battering as a rare
occurrence (51% vs. 35%).

Six out of ten Americans (57%) responding to the EDK survey also said they
believe that when a man and a woman fight there is a good chance he will grab
and shove her to make his point (24% said he did this often, and 33% said
sometimes). Women were perceived as less likely to use this level of physical
force with men (40% overall—11% believing she did this often, and 29% only
sometimes). This is not to say that women never express rage or anger in physical
ways. Although women do not usually physically abuse men, they do throw

TABLE 2.2 Percentage of Respondents Who Had Witnessed Violence in Private Relationships, by Sex and Race

	Says Nasty Things				Grabs and Shoves				Throws Something				Beats Badly			
	Male Perpetrator		Female Perpetrator		Male Perpetrator		Female Perpetrator		Male Perpetrator		Female Perpetrator		Male Perpetrator		Female Perpetrator	
	W	M	W	M	W	M	W	M	W	M	W	M	W	M	W	M
All	(48%)		(44%)		(24%)		(11%)		(13%)		(26%)		(19%)		(5%)	
Caucasians																
Often	53	42	49	39	26	17	13	8	17	9	28	19	22	13	7	4
Sometimes	31	36	32	37	34	33	30	28	27	24	31	29	30	21	10	9
Rarely	7	14	10	15	26	37	43	51	41	56	29	42	34	55	69	76
African Americans																
Often	34	35	27	33	25	19	14	12	13	14	18	25	21	18	8	10
Sometimes	29	25	28	33	29	31	33	32	32	33	34	31	21	15	18	10
Rarely	16	24	23	23	30	34	33	39	37	37	31	29	40	49	54	61
Latinos/as																
Often	50	45	47	35	33	25	21	24	21	18	32	29	39	27	10	7
Sometimes	36	33	35	39	33	36	34	29	31	34	29	39	25	33	20	17
Rarely	6	11	11	17	26	30	35	37	37	39	27	21	30	24	60	64
Asian Americans																
Often	50	48	46	41	31	21	16	10	23	12	23	22	25	16	8	6
Sometimes	30	29	34	36	38	44	38	39	36	33	41	34	32	32	14	16
Rarely	20	23	20	22	31	35	46	52	43	55	36	45	43	53	78	78

SOURCE: These data are from a 1992 poll conducted by EDK Associates, working with the Family Violence Prevention Fund. For details see Appendix B.
NOTE: W = women; M = men

things. And among EDK respondents, women were perceived as more likely to throw something at a man (55% overall—26% believing this happened often and 29% sometimes) than he is at her (39% overall—13% often and 26% sometimes).

Abusive behavior isn't only physical—men and women also verbally abuse each other. Almost half of the EDK respondents said that men often say nasty things to hurt women (48% felt this happened often and 11% only rarely). And in almost equal numbers, respondents thought women also say nasty things to hurt men (44% thought this happened often and 13% rarely).

Women respondents tended to acknowledge violent social behavior more often than men, independent of whether the perpetrator is male or female. For example, women were more likely than men to say that men grab and shove women at least sometimes (61% vs. 52%). They were also more likely to say that women grab and shove men sometimes (42% vs. 37%) (see Table 2.2).

Men respondents to the EDK poll were much more likely than women to say that throwing things at one another is a rarity, whether he is throwing things at her (56% vs. 41%) or vice versa (39% vs. 28%). Gender differences in the acknowledgment of violent behavior were most pronounced among Caucasians (see Table 2.2). Among this group, women reported greater frequency of violence than men: from the man being nasty to a woman (58% vs. 46%), to her being nasty to him (54% vs. 43%), to him often beating her (25% vs. 15%). Among Latinos, the most noteworthy difference was that whereas both men (64%) and women (70%) acknowledged that men beat women, Latinas were more likely than their male counterparts to say this happens often (42% vs. 28%). In contrast, Asian American men saw a greater prevalence of battering than Asian American women (57% vs. 48%). There were no gender differences in acknowledgment of violence among African Americans.

Caucasian men who responded to the EDK survey were the most resistant to acknowledging the physical threat men pose to women. They were much more likely to say that men *rarely* throw things at women (63%) than were African American men (50%), Latinos (45%), or Asian American men (41%). They were also more likely to deny that men beat women (62% of Caucasian men compared with 26% among Latinos, 53% among African American men, and 43% among Asian American men).

For the most part, perceptions concerning the prevalence of male violence toward women were not based on socioeconomic status. Once race and sex are taken into account in the EDK findings, there were few significant relationships based on either education or income in the perception of how often men grab and shove women, throw things at them, or resort to battering.

Caucasian men and women with more than a high school diploma were more likely to say men rarely grab and shove women than were those who did not complete high school (13% vs. 32% among women and 25% vs. 44% among men). Interestingly, there is a curvilinear relationship between education and the acknowledgment that men throw things: The percentage of EDK respondents who said this rarely happens increased from 42% among those without a high school degree to 72% for those with a high school diploma to 58% among the college-educated.

Within every race and ethnic group, there was no statistically significant relationship between perceptions of how often men beat women based on either education or income—and this was true independent of gender (see Table 2.3). For example, there was no statistical difference in the percentage of Caucasian men who said that men rarely beat women, whether the respondents came from households earning less than $15,000 a year (67%) or more than $45,000 a year (64%). Education did not make a statistically significant difference, either; men with a college degree (63%) were not statistically different in this regard from men with less than a high school degree (46%).

The Lieberman polls seem to indicate that American perceptions of the pervasiveness of domestic violence did not change dramatically in recent years, despite extensive media coverage on the issue—perhaps because the perceived level of violence was so high to begin with (see Table 2.4). Respondents in both July 1994 and November 1995 Lieberman polls were asked to estimate what percentage of men have ever physically abused their wives or girlfriends at least once, as a way of evaluating how widespread the problem is perceived to be. That perception remained virtually static in that time period, with respondents in both surveys estimating that one half of all men, on average, have physically abused their wives or girlfriends at one time or another.

There were important gender differences in the perception of the problem that did, however, change over time. Although men remained more likely than women to believe that the problem of domestic violence has been exaggerated by the media (31% vs. 19% in the November 1992 Lieberman poll), those numbers are lower, especially for men, than they were in the July 1994 poll, when 39% of men and 22% of women agreed with that statement.

It Happens to Us

Public recognition of the pervasiveness of domestic abuse reflects the level of violence that people acknowledge in their own lives. And although there have been important changes in the number of Americans willing to discuss the violence they have faced in recent years, even before this happened, the level of exposure to violence in Americans' lives was alarming (see Table 2.5). In 1992, the majority of respondents to the EDK survey (57%) reported having witnessed potentially violent circumstances. Men had witnessed violence even more than women (63% vs. 50%). More people had directly witnessed an incidence of domestic violence (34%) and child abuse (23%) than had witnessed muggings and robberies combined (19%). Thus one out of three American men and women had stared domestic violence in the face. And although family violence was not shown to be limited to men beating women (2 out of 10 men reported having witnessed a woman beating up her husband or boyfriend), most respondents identified men beating women as a very serious problem.

Perhaps this is true because of the apparent prevalence of this form of violence—in the 1992 EDK poll, some 14% of women respondents acknowledged having been abused by a husband or boyfriend. In the polling conducted by Lieberman Research immediately after the arrest of O. J. Simpson and the media coverage that ensued (July 1994), 24% of women respondents reported having been physically abused by a husband or boyfriend at some point in their lives. Perhaps most strikingly, that proportion increased to 31% in the Lieberman poll conducted between November 1994 and February 1995, less than a year later (see Table 2.6).

In the November 1995 Lieberman poll, the incidence of reported domestic violence was greatest among lower- and middle-income women (household

TABLE 2.3 Percentage of Respondents Who Believe Men Beat Women: By Race, Gender, and Class

	Men			Women		
	Often	Sometimes	Rarely	Often	Sometimes	Rarely
Caucasian						
Education						
< High school	25	29	46	26	29	45
High school	13	23	64	29	37	34
Some college	19	18	63	22	34	43
College+	10	27	63	24	35	42
Income[a]						
< $15,000	12	21	67	20	34	46
$15,000 to $24,999	22	22	56	33	26	42
$25,000 to $34,999	14	21	65	19	43	38
$35,000 to $44,999	13	20	67	36	29	36
$45,000+	8	29	64	18	39	43
African American						
Education						
< High school	14	29	57	33	23	43
High school	17	19	53	33	41	26
Some college	23	33	44	29	23	48
College+	45	15	60	25	15	60
Income[a]						
< $15,000	24	21	56	36	27	36
$15,000 to $24,999	33	25	43	30	24	46
$25,000+	10	28	63	17	35	48
Latinos						
Education						
< High school	34	26	40	33	27	39
High school	33	41	26	51	31	19
Some college	44	40	37	40	26	34
College+	19	34	47	35	24	41
Income[a]						
< $15,000	37	26	28	45	26	29
$15,000 to $24,999	33	40	28	50	17	33
$25,000+	16	30	54	40	30	30

income less than $40,000), 35- to 49-year-olds, and small town/rural and city residents. There was a substantial increase in reports of physical abuse among middle-income women (household income of $20,000 to $39,000): While in the November 1994-February 1995 poll, 26% of middle-income women reported having been physically abused at some point in their lives, that number skyrocketed to 41% by November 1995. This may be a result of media coverage of

TABLE 2.3 *Continued*

	Men			Women		
	Often	*Sometimes*	*Rarely*	*Often*	*Sometimes*	*Rarely*
Asian American						
Education						
< High school	23	39	39	18	27	55
High school	31	31	39	14	43	43
Some college	19	38	43	18	37	46
College+	25	27	48	14	27	59
Income[a]						
< $15,000	28	28	45	14	29	57
$15,000 to $24,999	38	19	44	18	29	53
$25,000+	24	32	44	12	28	60

SOURCE: These data are from a 1992 poll conducted by EDK Associates, working with the Family Violence Prevention Fund. For details see Appendix B.

NOTE: There were no statistically significant differences in responses based on education or income, and this was true independent of gender.

a. Note that there are more categories of income for Caucasians than for other groups. This is due in part to the smaller sample size of the African American, Hispanic, and Asian American groups.

Nicole Brown Simpson's battery, one of the most highly publicized cases involving an upper-middle-class victim of spousal abuse.

To obtain another perspective on the incidence of domestic violence, Lieberman survey respondents were also asked if they knew any women who had been physically abused by their husbands or boyfriends. As discussed in Chapter 1, there has been a consistent increase in the percentage of people saying they *know* an abused woman since July 1994 (see Table 2.7). In the most recent poll for which results are available (November 1995), more than one third of respondents reported that they knew women who were victims of physical abuse (35%). This number is a dramatic increase from results obtained in July 1994, when 29% believed they knew a victim. This increase may indicate that in the current climate, women who are abused are more willing to talk about their experiences.

The likelihood of knowing an abused woman is greatest among women, 18- to 34-year-olds, middle-income households ($20,000 to $39,999), and city residents. These groups also show significant increases in knowing physically abused women over the course of the Lieberman polling.

These dramatic changes in such a short time period—a time period during which there was an unprecedented amount of media coverage on the issue of domestic violence in outlets across the country—support the notion that public

TABLE 2.4 Changing Perceptions About the Number of Men Who Have Ever Physically Abused Wives or Girlfriends

	Percentage of Respondents in:			
Number of Men[a]	July 1994 (N = 735)	January-February 1995[b] (N = 486)	November 1995 (N = 742)	January-February 1995 Versus November 1995
Most men	7	9	10	+1
More than one half	23	19	21	+2
About one half	30	32	31	−1
Less than one half	28	27	25	−2
Only a few men	7	8	8	±0
Don't know	5	5	5	±0
Mean percentage	49	49	50	+1

SOURCE: These data are from polls conducted by Lieberman Research, Inc., working with the Family Violence Prevention Fund and The Advertising Council. For details see Appendix C.

a. The categories in this column were read to respondents, and they were asked to choose one.

b. The second wave of polling by Lieberman Research took place from November 1994 to February 1995. However, data from the shorter January-February period were used here so that they would be more comparable to the first- and third-wave polls, which were conducted in a single month.

education campaigns on the issue of domestic violence help provide a climate in which women who have faced this problem can talk about it more openly.

In Their Own Words: Focus Group Findings

Data gathered in the focus groups corroborate findings about the prevalence of domestic violence in Americans' lives. The people attending the groups were not selected on the basis of their exposure to incidents of violence, nor were they told that the subject matter to be discussed was domestic violence. Therefore, the proportion of people in these groups who volunteered personal stories of intimate partner violence was quite striking.

Of the white women who told stories about their own experiences with domestic violence, four had family members who were abused and two had family members who were abusers. "I put up with it at first," confided one white woman from Little Rock, who had not attended college.

At first it was yelling, verbal attacks. Then it was the jealousy. I couldn't go to the grocery store without [my first husband] being afraid I was going to meet

TABLE 2.5 Percentage of Respondents Who Reported Personal Exposure to Violence

	All	*Women*	*Men*
Have you ever witnessed people yelling loudly at each another and threatening to get violent?	57	50	63
Were you ever in such a screaming match?	20	19	21
Did you worry about the other person becoming violent?	16	17	15
Did you worry that you might get violent?	11	9	13
Have you ever witnessed a man beating his wife or girlfriend?	34	33	35
Has a husband or boyfriend ever beaten your mother or your stepmother?	7	8	5
Has a husband or boyfriend ever been violent with you?	NA	14	NA
Have you ever witnessed a woman beating her husband or boyfriend?[a]	16	10	20
Has a wife or girlfriend ever been violent with you?	NA	NA	7
Have you ever witnessed a parent beating a child?[a]	23	20	25
Were you or any of your brothers or sisters beaten as a child?	8	7	8
Have you ever witnessed a robbery or mugging?	19	12	25
Were you ever robbed or mugged?	11	8	14

SOURCE: These data are from a 1992 poll conducted by EDK Associates, working with the Family Violence Prevention Fund. For details see Appendix B.

NOTE: The indented questions were only asked of those who said yes to the first question in each section.

a. Gender differences significant at $p = .05$.

some man that had money. So I went through many months before it got physical. The physical wasn't as bad as what I've seen other women have. Mine was a slap across the face, and he hit me hard enough to cause me to fall down the stairs. So it wasn't as brutal as some women have had it, but it was bad enough that I felt completely emotionally and physically beat up.

White men in the focus groups talked about colleagues, wives, and girlfriends who had been beaten by former husbands, and a few even admitted to past acts of violence.

TABLE 2.6 Percentage of Women Reporting Physical Abuse by a Spouse or
Boyfriend: Demographic Changes Over Time

	July 1994	November 1994-February 1995	November 1995	November 1994-February 1995 Versus November 1995	(Average Base)
Total	24	31	30	−1	(412)
California	35	35	29	−6	(115)
Age					
18 to 34 years	26	34	27	−7[a]	(165)
35 to 49 years	24	34	37	+3	(150)
50 to 65 years	20	20	28	+8	(91)
Household income					
< $20,000	38	45	39	−6	(90)
$20,000 to $39,999	28	26	41	+15[b]	(121)
$40,000 or more	10	23	20	−3	(138)
Type of area					
City	40	42	34	−8	(108)
Suburban	17	29	20	−9[a]	(133)
Small town/rural	18	27	36	+9	(169)

SOURCE: These data are from polls conducted by Lieberman Research, Inc., working with the Family
Violence Prevention Fund and The Advertising Council. For details see Appendix C.

a. Significantly lower at a 95% confidence level.

b. Significantly higher at a 95% confidence level.

We had really physical fights. Throwing things. She was a very physical person.
She'd start throwing things and hitting me and eventually I'd just slap the shit
out of her. [Group laughter]

> White man (Dallas);
> some college education or more

Several African American women talked about being abused by their ex-
husbands. Others admitted having a family member or close friend who was
being abused at the time.

My first husband knew my father didn't rear me, so in his mind, he felt that he
was going to show me how a man is in the home. Whenever I said or did
something that he didn't like, well, he would just hit me. [Moderator: And then
you would . . .] Hit him back. That's really the reason I got out of the
marriage—because of the physical abuse. I felt like he was like that with me
because he saw his dad with his mom. That's what I honestly believe.

> African American woman (Los Angeles);
> high school graduate or some college education

TABLE 2.7 Percentage of Respondents Who Know Women Who Are Physically Abused: Demographic Changes Over Time

	July 1994	November 1994-February 1995	November 1995	November 1994-February 1995 Versus November 1995	(Average Base)
Total	29	33	35	+2	(820)
California	32	38	37	−1	(229)
Gender					
Female	32	40	42	+2	(412)
Male	26	25	28	+3	(408)
Age					
18 to 34 years	35	32	41	+9[a]	(333)
35 to 49 years	30	35	33	−2	(303)
50 to 65 years	17	28	24	−4	(176)
Household income					
< $20,000	33	40	34	−6	(161)
$20,000 to $39,999	32	28	46	+18[a]	(239)
$40,000 or more	25	35	31	−4	(303)
Type of area					
City	37	28	42	+14[a]	(210)
Suburban	30	32	33	+1	(278)
Small town/rural	24	36	33	−3	(329)

SOURCE: These data are from polls conducted by Lieberman Research, Inc., working with the Family Violence Prevention Fund and The Advertising Council. For details see Appendix C.

a. Significantly higher at a 95% confidence interval.

African American men reluctantly admitted that family violence is a real problem in the black community. Two mentioned that their fathers beat their mothers. One talked about his grandmother having been abused, and another was troubled that his young daughter had witnessed the abuse of her next-door neighbor.

> I was over at my daughter's house. Her mother was telling me that the next-door neighbor's boyfriend had gotten out of jail, and he was out there beating on his girlfriend, and my daughter was out there seeing all that stuff. She came and said, "Mama, you should see this—he slap her down and she said, 'Stop it,' and he just kept slapping her down."
>
> African American man (Los Angeles);
> high school graduate or some college education

Both Latinas and Latinos were also worried about the prevalence of violence. Three of the women had family members who were abused, two were beaten by their fathers while growing up, and one woman currently had an abusive boyfriend. Three of the women also expressed fear that their husbands could become violent.

> My husband's father hit his wife and they separated. I think something has to do with the family. And my husband is violent. I try not to get him violent.
>
> Latina (Los Angeles);
> some college education or less

Among Latinos, group members made references to a sister being beaten, a cousin who abused his wife, and a friend who beat his girlfriend. Several mentioned that their girlfriends pushed them near violence, and one said he was "forced to" slap his girlfriend to "keep her in line."

> I had a friend who had these problems. The girl was making more money, and she was just putting down the guy. She would destroy that person. There is nothing he could feel nice about. A couple of times that person beat up this girl because he got to a point, he got so mad. She was pushing and pushing.
>
> Latino (Los Angeles);
> some college education or less

Survey Findings in the Context of Prior Research

The domestic violence prevalence results reported here are consistent with prior incidence studies on the same subject. The first national random (probability) survey on domestic violence was conducted by Murray Straus, Richard Gelles, and Suzanne Steinmetz in 1978 (Straus et al., 1980) and repeated in 1985 (Straus & Gelles, 1990). The most recent Straus and Gelles (1990) national Family Violence Survey (FVS) revealed a 16% annual incidence of couples experiencing at least one episode of physical violence during the previous year, and a 3.4% incidence of serious forms of assault by males against female partners, defined by the researchers as wife beating.

The other major survey of note is the National Victim Survey (NVS; Bachman, 1994; Bachman & Saltzman, 1995), which examined wife assault from the criminal justice perspective. The NVS again used excellent telephone survey techniques, including appropriate oversampling of the major ethnic groups. In an earlier version of the survey, in order for a battered woman to be counted, she first had to self-identify as a victim of a crime—and, starting in 1994, as a victim of violence. However, the majority of battered women from the community (not from shelters or clinical populations) do not consider their experiences of violent acts at the hands of their intimate partners to be abuse or battering, let alone a crime (J. C. Campbell et al., 1994). A battered woman's recognition that what happened to her could be defined as a crime—or even as violence—usually comes after she has left the abusive relationship and is in a process of recovery from the abuse (Landenburger, 1989). Therefore, the results of the NVS reflect only those battered women who were most severely abused or who had decided that their abusive experience was indeed a crime. Consequently, the incidence of domestic violence from the NVS (5.4 per 1,000 or just over .05%) was far less than the FVS (16%). Discrepancies may be accounted for by the fact that the NVS asked one question using the words "victimized by violence," whereas the FVS asked about gradually escalating conflict tactics, beginning with words like "discussion" and then querying about "pushing and shoving."

Data examining *lifetime* rates of domestic violence consistently measure significant numbers. In the 1978 FVS, there was a 28% rate of respondents *ever* having been pushed or shoved by a partner, 18% of *ever* having been slapped, and 9% of *ever* having been hit or punched (prevalence data not reported for the 1985 survey). In response to the EDK survey in 1992, 14% of women said their husband or boyfriend had been violent with them at some point. The Lieberman polls also measured high rates of violence—in July 1994, 24% of women said they had been physically abused by their husbands or boyfriends at some point in their lives—and by November 1995, that proportion was up to 30% (28% of whom reported that the abuse happened frequently, whereas 57% reported it happened frequently or occasionally), perhaps because of the more supportive climate that existed for victims of domestic violence at that time. It should be noted that prevalence determination was not the major aim of the FVS, EDK, or Lieberman polls—yet these are nevertheless useful estimates of how wide-spread the problem is.

Canadian researchers (Johnson & Sacco, 1995) also conducted a national random survey specifically to address violence against women. They framed their questions in that context, rather than around conflict resolution or crime. This carefully constructed and administered survey is an important model for a recently completed survey jointly funded by the U.S. Centers for Disease for Control and the National Institute of Justice. In the Canadian survey, the overall prevalence of domestic violence (women ever physically and/or sexually assaulted by an intimate partner or ex-partner) was 29%, whereas 15% had been assaulted by their current partner sometime in the relationship, and 5% by a partner or ex-partner within the prior year. These data suggest that the degree of victimization from spouses is similar in the United States and Canada. The survey also indicates that in Canada (as in the United States), women are more likely to be victimized by a current or former intimate partner than by a stranger.

Gender and Incidence Rates

Data from the early surveys, including the FVS (Straus & Gelles, 1990; Straus et al., 1980), seem to indicate that women use violent tactics in relationships as often as men do. However, these studies used the Conflict Tactics Scale (CTS), which does not distinguish between violent tactics used in self-defense and those used as the first aggressive tactic (Saunders, 1986).

Even so, most experts (including Gelles and Straus) agree that women are far more likely to be hurt in violent relationships and that men tend to underreport their rates of severe violence. The gender differences in severe intimate partner violence are perhaps more accurately depicted by the NVS (Bachman, 1994; Bachman & Saltzman, 1995), which uses differently worded questions. Ten times as many women as men in that survey said they had been victims of intimate partner violence serious enough to be considered a crime (Bachman, 1994).

There is much evidence based on prior research that husbands and wives do not agree on the frequency and severity of violent tactics used by male partners in intimate relationships (Edleson & Brygger, 1986; Jouriles & O'Leary, 1985; Szinovacz, 1983). The EDK polling results from 1992 reflect this tendency: When asked whether or not they had witnessed a woman beating her husband or boyfriend, 16% of all respondents said they had—but the gender split was noteworthy, with 10% of women and 20% of men agreeing. In another gender difference, women tended to be painfully honest about how much violence they use, whereas men, at least abusive men, tended to underestimate the extent of their violence and the damage it inflicts.

Another relevant demographic finding from the NVS (Bachman, 1994; Bachman & Saltzman, 1995) and the Canadian Survey (Johnson & Sacco, 1995) is that significantly more separated and divorced women reported experiencing serious intimate violence than married or single women. The marital status result probably reflects three very different dynamics, but it is impossible from the data to determine which is the major cause. Data from both battered women advocates, reports on clinical experience, and other sources (e.g., Wilson, Johnson, & Daly, 1993) show that women often experience increased violence after they leave a violent intimate relationship. The marital status finding may also reflect the fact that while they are still married, women might be less likely to define their experience as a crime because they continue to be invested in making the relationship work. Yet, if women have left the relationship, their mental construction of the experience often shifts, and they are more likely to define the violence as a criminal assault. The difference may also reflect the possibility that separated and divorced women may report violence in a relationship with a new partner with whom they are living. The 1985 FVS also found a significantly greater rate of violence among cohabiting couples than among those who are married (Straus & Gelles, 1990).

Race/Ethnicity

The NVS (Bachman, 1994) depicts a different ethnic and marital status breakdown from the FVS, with the proportion of African American, Anglo, and Latina women affected by serious domestic violence not significantly different. (Asian Americans were not sufficiently sampled in either the FVS or the NVS to analyze the results separately.) In the FVS, significantly higher proportions of Hispanic and African American men were violent (both in terms of minor and severe tactics) toward their wives than were Anglo men, but these differences are mitigated and/or disappear when economic deprivation, urban residence, and comparative youth are controlled for (Straus & Gelles, 1990). Thus the fact that few ethnic differences were found may well be based on reality, but the Anglo male reluctance to acknowledge the widespread prevalence of men beating women is of concern, especially given the ongoing power this group holds in effecting societal change.

Change Over Time

Evidence exists that public perception about domestic violence has changed drastically over time and that the actual occurrence of severe violence decreased between the 1978 FVS (Straus et al., 1980) and the 1985 FVS (Straus & Gelles, 1990). However, the difference was not statistically significant. It may have reflected a diminishing public tolerance for wife beating. Perhaps people were less willing to admit to violence over the phone (even in an anonymous survey), or they might have been less likely actually to commit violent acts against their spouse. In either case, the changes are heartening.

Why Does Domestic Violence Happen?

It is both public perception and reality that men frequently grab, push, shove, and punch women. To build support for social remedies, the EDK survey in 1992 tried to determine *why* people think violence against women happens. We found that most people did not really know why men beat women. *But they agreed that no matter what the reason, it is wrong.*

Participants in the EDK focus groups were asked "Why do men beat women?" Many people reacted with a long pause or asked us to clarify the question. Some attempted to shift the focus to the previous conversation. Others shied away from answering the direct question. Perhaps the subject was too personal and too difficult. Researchers themselves find it difficult to explain domestic violence. Despite years of study, the answers are not clear and the evidence is contradictory. As is the case with other social problems, the reasons for domestic violence are complex and not easily solved. Ambiguity makes people uncomfortable. We want clear-cut answers.

The EDK survey offered respondents two chances to answer the question of why men are violent toward women. The first opportunity was an open-ended question. People were asked to imagine that a woman whom they knew was beaten up by her husband or boyfriend. They were then asked why they thought he did this. The single most common answer was "I don't know." Men were significantly more likely than women to say they did not know (33% to 26%) (see Table 3.1).

These responses suggest that there was still a residual tendency to believe that he could not help his violence (35%): He was drunk, was sick, or didn't know how to communicate. About 20% said he did it to control her, to keep her

TABLE 3.1 Why Men Beat Women: Responses to Open-Ended Question

	Percentage of Respondents		
	All	*Women*	*Men*
Suppose I told you a woman you knew was beaten up by her husband or boyfriend. Why do you think he did it?			
Don't know	29	26	33
He couldn't help it	35	37	31
He was drunk and did not know what he was doing	14	14	13
He didn't know how to communicate	12	13	11
He is sick, disturbed, violent	9	10	7
He did it to control her	18	21	17
He wanted to keep her in line/get her to do what he wants	9	11	8
He has bad self-esteem and is taking it out on her	10	10	9
She asked for it	12	8	14
She provoked it by yelling, screaming, and hitting him	5	4	5
She cheated on him	7	4	9
He learned it at home	5	6	4

SOURCE: These data are from a 1992 poll conducted by EDK Associates, working with the Family Violence Prevention Fund. For details see Appendix B.

in line. Only 12% blamed the victim, saying she provoked him or cheated on him. Unlike the focus group discussions, which were filled with references to violent episodes participants had seen while they were growing up, most people in the telephone poll did not spontaneously mention childhood learning as a causal factor.

In another portion of the survey, respondents were given a set of explanations of why a man would beat a woman and then asked to choose which came closest to their view (see Table 3.2). The "don't know" response dropped from 29% in the open-ended question to 8% overall. Instead, one out of three respondents (34%) said they believed a man would beat a woman in order to control her. Almost one in four (23%) said they believed he would do this because he was beaten when he was young or saw his mother being abused, and one in five (20%) thought it was because he was drunk and did not mean to do it. Few people thought the man was acting out cultural images depicting violence (10%) or purposefully trying to rob the woman of her self-esteem (6%).

The EDK survey data demonstrated significant gender differences in terms of how people explain why a man would beat a woman. Men were more likely than women to say he beat her because he was drunk and out of control (25% of men versus 16% of women), whereas women were more likely to say he learned it when he was young (27% of women vs. 19% of men).

TABLE 3.2 Why Men Beat Women: Responses to Multiple Choice Question

	Percentage of Respondents		
	All	*Women*	*Men*
Which of the following comes closest to your view of why a man would beat a woman?			
He got drunk/lost control	20	16	25
He was beaten when he was young	23	27	19
He is acting out cultural images	8	9	8
He wants to control her	34	35	33
He's trying to rob her of self-esteem	6	6	5

SOURCE: These data are from a 1992 poll conducted by EDK Associates, working with the Family Violence Prevention Fund. For details see Appendix B.

Age, income, and education also influenced answers given in the EDK survey. Age was a factor among men but not women. Older men were most likely to agree with the "he got drunk" argument (36% compared with 25% among men overall). Income and education shaped women's responses but not men's. Women from households earning less than $25,000 a year were more likely to say he beat her because he wants to control her, whereas women from higher-income households were more likely to say he was beaten when he was young. Women with a high school education at most were more likely to say it was an issue of his wanting to control her than were those women with some college education (see Table 3.3).

Most respondents to the EDK survey had not spent much time thinking about why there is violence against women. One way researchers measure how central an idea or explanation is to people is to look at how consistently they respond to other questions tapping a similar theme. In the EDK poll, in addition to there being no clear explanation for the problem of domestic violence given in the unguided questions, there was also a high degree of inconsistency between the reasons given when the question was first asked without any structured answers and when the participants were given a choice. Two thirds of the people who gave one answer to the unstructured question later gave a different response when asked which statement came closest to their view of why men beat women (see Table 3.4).

For example, when respondents were asked the unstructured question, 37% of white women said a man beats a woman because he is drunk, doesn't know how to communicate, or is sick. When later given a series of reasons to explain domestic violence, their answers changed: 20% said a man would beat a woman because he got drunk or lost control (their original answer); 27% said it was a matter of having learned it at home; and 35% said he wanted to control her (the opposite end of the spectrum from their original answer). We found a similar pattern for men.

TABLE 3.3 Why Men Beat Women: Multiple Choice Responses by
Demographic Group

| | *Percentage of Respondents Who Chose:* | | | | | | | |
| | *He Got Drunk/ Lost Control* | | *He Was Beaten When He Was Young* | | *He Is Acting Out Cultural Images* | | *He Wants to Control Her* | |
	Women	*Men*	*Women*	*Men*	*Women*	*Men*	*Women*	*Men*
All	15	25	27	19	9	8	35	33
Age[a]								
18 to 24	13	28	28	17	13	7	39	37
25 to 34	16	21	29	27	7	10	35	28
35 to 44	11	17	27	26	11	7	33	34
45 to 54	17	24	37	8	7	8	30	41
55+	21	35	32	13	8	9	29	25
Income[b]								
< $15,000	19	30	23	14	8	12	41	35
$15,000 to 25,000	16	22	27	20	7	5	37	38
$25,000 to 35,000	17	24	36	24	4	8	35	23
$35,000 to 45,000	12	26	36	19	12	7	21	33
$45,000+	c	20	33	27	29	c	31	21
Education[d]								
< High school	23	30	25	9	4	13	34	33
High school graduate	18	27	25	20	6	6	42	29
Some college	17	26	17	18	11	8	8	36
College graduate	10	20	39	28	11	7	25	31
Postgraduate	12	20	51	12	12	12	21	35

SOURCE: These data are from a 1992 poll conducted by EDK Associates, working with the Family Violence Prevention Fund. For details see Appendix B.

a. Differences in men's responses are significant at $p = .01$. Differences in women's responses are nonsignificant.

b. Differences in women's responses are significant at $p = .06$. Differences in men's responses are nonsignificant.

c. Too small a number for comparison.

d. Differences in women's responses are significant at $p = .00$. Differences in men's responses are nonsignificant.

Communication and Gender-Related American Norms

A popular belief about domestic violence is that the absence of productive communication is one of the reasons for family violence. Most Americans concur that men are often socialized to view violence as an acceptable way to resolve conflict. Thus reducing domestic violence requires a stronger societal message that stresses the unacceptability of male violence against females.

Many men grow up learning to be aggressive—yelling and fighting are part of how they get their way. Women typically learn to be expressive—talking about feelings is their primary way of being understood. In the EDK poll, participants believed that men and women have different patterns of communication and that

TABLE 3.4 Why Men Beat Women: Comparison of Responses to Open-Ended and Multiple Choice Questions

He Beats Her Because:	He Got Drunk/ Lost Control	He Was Beaten When He Was Young	He Is Acting Out Cultural Images/ Aggressiveness	He's Trying to Rob Her of Her Self-Esteem	He Wants to Control Her	Don't Know
Women						
All	16%	27%	9%	6%	25%	6%
He couldn't help it (37%)	20	27	8	5	35	5
He wants to control her (21%)	9	23	10	6	49	3
She asked for it (8%)	22	30	6	—	39	2
He learned it at home (6%)	—	58	3	7	29	3
Don't know (26%)	19	24	11	9	25	13
Men						
All						
He couldn't help it (37%)	20	27	8	5	35	5
He wants to control her (21%)	9	23	10	6	49	3
She asked for it (8%)	22	30	6	—	39	2
He learned it at home (6%)	—	58	3	7	29	3
Don't know (26%)	19	24	11	9	25	3

SOURCE: These data are from a 1992 poll conducted by EDK Associates, working with the Family Violence Prevention Fund. For details see Appendix B.

NOTE: An interesting feature of this survey was that respondents often gave different replies to the open-ended and multiple choice versions of questions about why men beat women. The open-ended responses are in the left-hand column, with the percentage who gave each reply in parentheses. The multiple choice responses are at the tops of the columns. The numbers in the columns are the percentages of those who gave each open-ended response who also made the selection at the head of the column.

they use different techniques to get their way. People recognized that both men and women can be manipulative to get their way. But men and women agreed that many men have serious problems with a need to control and an inability to express themselves (see Table 3.5).

The EDK survey respondents were asked whether they agreed with a series of statements that characterized the emotional context of male-female relationships. First, we asked about women: Did they agree that women often want men to take care of them? that women cry to get their way? that they are too emotional? or that they expect too much from men? Then we asked about men: Did they agree that men expect too much from women? that they often want to

TABLE 3.5 The Communication Gap: Gender Differences in Agreement With Beliefs About Men's and Women's Behavior

	Percentage of Respondents		
Statement/Response	All	Women	Men
Women often want men to take care of them.			
Strongly agree	39	38	41
Agree	39	41	37
Disagree	15	15	15
Strongly disagree	5	6	5
Women often cry to get their way.			
Strongly agree	20	18	22
Agree	39	38	40
Disagree	24	24	24
Strongly disagree	14	17	10
Women are too emotional.			
Strongly agree	21	22	21
Agree	33	31	34
Disagree	28	27	28
Strongly disagree	15	17	13
Women expect too much from men.			
Strongly agree	17	17	17
Agree	27	25	29
Disagree	33	31	35
Strongly disagree	19	22	16
Men expect too much from women.			
Strongly agree	30	36	24
Agree	32	30	34
Disagree	24	22	27
Strongly disagree	10	8	11
Men often want to be in control.			
Strongly agree	59	65	54
Agree	29	26	32
Disagree	29	26	32
Strongly disagree	6	6	7
Men need to learn how to express themselves.[a]			
Strongly agree	61	69	52
Agree	29	22	36
Disagree	6	6	6
Strongly disagree	3	2	4
Men think they can solve everything by yelling.			
Strongly agree	18	23	13
Agree	25	25	25
Disagree	33	32	34
Strongly disagree	20	16	25

SOURCE: These data are from a 1992 poll conducted by EDK Associates, working with the Family Violence Prevention Fund. For details see Appendix B.

NOTE: Differences significant at $p = .00$. All other differences are nonsignificant.

be in control? that they need to learn how to express themselves? and that they think they can solve everything by yelling?

We found that EDK survey respondents perceived men's need to control and their inability to express themselves as underlying the violence in intimate relationships between men and women. The two most salient statements of this set of questions—the ones with the largest strong agreement—were "Men need to learn to express themselves" (felt by 69% of women and 52% of men, a 17-point difference in saliency) and "Men often want to be in control" (felt by 65% of women and 54% of men, an 11-point difference). Women were more likely than men to agree that men think they can solve everything by yelling (48% vs. 38%). Both sexes agreed that men need to learn how to express themselves, but women were more likely than men to agree strongly with this sentiment (69% vs. 52%). Neither income nor education had a significant impact on how strongly men or women agreed with these statements.

A significant part of the EDK focus group conversation in all ethnic groups centered around the general nature of men's and women's failure to learn how to communicate with each another.

Men don't talk. We could sit here and talk until 12 tonight. But men, it will take you years to get things out of them. They want to get along with you and they think that talking will disturb the relationship.

> African American woman (Los Angeles);
> high school graduate or some college

When we get frustrated, we just talk it out with someone else. Men don't. They just keep [it] inside.

> White woman (Hartford);
> some college education or more

Men always have this thing about hiding their true feelings. Even if they love their women, they still don't let it all hang out. I put a lot of time, energy, and effort into this relationship, and in my mind I want it to work and be good, so why don't you verbalize it, express it, let her know?

> African American man (Los Angeles);
> high school graduate or some college

I think most Asian men don't talk about their feelings, or I don't think they talk about problems and things. At least, in my family, my brother-in-law, my brother.

> Asian woman (San Francisco);
> high school or college graduate

It's the way boys and girls grew up fighting. Boys are physical when they grow up. We don't scream at each other. If we scream, we get into a fist fight. Boys try to reason, to get along. If they get into a confrontation, they're either going to reach an agreement or get into a fight. That's the way we operate. But girls talk rough at each other, give each other dirty looks and scream at each other, and cat fight. So when we get into relationships, they start that with us, and we are not used to standing there for long periods of hollering, screaming—they're gritting their teeth and giving dirty looks. We lose our temper after a while because in all the time growing up, it was either walk away or fight.

White man (Dallas); some college education or more

Some men believe that women expect too much from men and that this leads to confusion and ultimately violence.

[Women expect too much from men.] They want us to be Rhett Butler and Ashley Wilkes at the same time. They want me to be the sensitive, sweet, caring, soft-spoken guy and then get out and whip 12 guys if they bother us at a football game. They want me to understand all their whims. I don't believe men want that much from women. We can't be all the things ladies want us to be.

White man (Dallas);
some college education or more

Regarding expectations, however, many more people said that men expect too much from women (62%), compared with those who said women expect too much from men (44%). The gender differences in response to these assertions were remarkably small. Only slightly more women than men agreed that men expect too much from women (66% of women vs. 58% of men). Women were as likely as men to agree that they expect too much from men (42% vs. 46%).

Violence Is Learned

Most Americans think violence is learned at home. People believe that when there is violence in the family, it sets up a chain of violence that often, but not always, repeats itself: A man who beats a woman most likely has seen his father beat his mother and is repeating this behavior with his girlfriend, wife, and next wife. His children learn from him and their children learn from them. The cycle is endless. Researchers generally find that the data agree with public perception. However, they warn that exposure to violence as a child does not explain all of domestic violence (Straus & Gelles, 1990).

In the EDK survey, we found that respondents strongly agreed that some people learned to be violent because when they were young, they were beaten or witnessed violence in their homes (see Table 3.5). Across race, class, and ethnic groups, people strongly agreed with this statement. There was significantly stronger agreement among Caucasian women compared with Caucasian men (57% of women strongly agreed compared with 44% of men, a 13-point difference) and among Latinas compared with Latinos (41% vs. 27%, a 14-point difference). Latinos were least likely to strongly agree (27%), but still, overall, 60% agreed. African American men were more likely than African American women to disagree with this statement (20% vs. 12%). There was no gender difference among Asian Americans.

Age and education did interact with race and gender. In the EDK poll, Caucasian women under 45 were significantly more likely to agree strongly that violence was learned in childhood than those 45 years and older. Education was an important factor for Caucasian women, as well. Those with college degrees were in stronger agreement than those with less than a college education. And African American men were much more likely to agree with this statement if they had some college education or more (see Table 3.6).

Focus group respondents also indicated that people felt this was a viable explanation for why men beat women.

It's because that's what they know. That's all they have seen. They can get away with it. [Lots of agreement from other participants.]

White woman (Hartford);
some college education or more

A lot of how you reckon your relationship today is how your parents reacted and how you and your parents interacted. That has a lot to do with how you deal with your spouse and kids.

White man (Dallas);
some college education or more

I know what happened. He was threatened. He was out of work. House payments were behind. She was barely holding a part-time job. They have three sons. A baby who is only a year-and-a-half. There was a lot of trouble. This is what he saw when he was a child to react to this stress.

Latina (Los Angeles);
some college education or less

My husband's father hit his wife and they separated. I think something has to do with the family. And my husband is violent. I try not to get him violent. . . . I

TABLE 3.6 Percentage of Respondents Who Strongly Agree That Men Who Beat Their Wives Learned to Be Violent as Children, by Demographic Group

	Caucasians		African Americans		Latinos/ Latinas		Asian Americans	
	Women	Men	Women	Men	Women	Men	Women	Men
All	57	44	35	33	41	27	51	49
Age								
18 to 24	64[a]	47	45[b]	35[c]	39	33[d]	35	24
25 to 34	63	45	36	32	47	20	39	42
35 to 44	67	45	39	43	33	38	38	42
45 to 54	58	42	43	44	42	14	33	38
55 and over	39	42	26	24	36	21	21	38
p	.00	NS	.08	.05	NS	.07	NS	NS
Education								
< High school	41[a]	42	33[d]	21[e]	23	25	42	28
High school graduate	49	40	29	28	42	25	33	44
Some college	52	51	42	37	50	31	27	34
College graduate	74	42	43	41	43	29	35	39
Postgraduate	75	40	50	57	50	20	45	44
p	.00	NS	.07	.02	NS	NS	NS	NS

SOURCE: These data are from a 1992 poll conducted by EDK Associates, working with the Family Violence Prevention Fund. For details see Appendix B.

NOTE: The exact wording of the survey statement is: "Beating up on women is often learned in the home. Some people learn to be violent because when they were young, they were beaten or witnessed violence in their home." The following *p* values are for age and education differences within gender and racial groups. Where no *p* value is given, any differences are nonsignificant.

a. $p = .00$.
b. $p = .08$.
c. $p = .05$.
d. $p = .07$.
e. $p = .02$

can't talk to him—yell at him when I want to tell him something. I can't, but he can. He tells me to be quiet. I have to be quiet, because I'm afraid he might hit me.

> Latina (Los Angeles);
> some college education or less

The link between battering and juvenile delinquency was a powerful one for the Los Angeles focus group participants, where gangs were a major concern, as well as in Dallas, where both white men and African American women worried about crime. Both the men and women in these groups wanted to save the children. The African American men spoke about the kids who were potential gang members as "their kids." They were worried about losing another generation. Saving these kids was the number one reason people wanted to intervene to stop men from beating women.

> The rage and anger in the gangs is from young men whose father[s] beat their mothers and abandoned them when they were kids. That's the anger and the rage. You got the violence.
>
> Latino (Los Angeles);
> some college education or less

In the EDK survey, both Asian American men and women agreed that children are influenced by the violent behavior they witness in their parents. However, Asian men were slightly more apt to agree strongly that violence is learned in the home (41% of men compared with 32% of women). Here are some typical replies from the focus groups.

> They are the result of their parents' actions. It was OK to beat up somebody in some cases, or it was OK to be beaten by somebody in some cases. I think it says it's OK because kids, at least my daughter, and she's only 3, mimics us. I think a lot of that is instilled from the ground up. It's OK to be violent.
>
> Asian man (San Francisco);
> high school graduate or some college

> I think some of it is learned, you know, when the child saw the parents doing that, and when they grew up and to them it was just life and so they did it. They may not realize why they are doing it; they are just thinking on the circumstances similar to what they saw and learned.
>
> Asian woman (San Francisco);
> high school graduate or some college

Cultural Images

The EDK survey shows that the public prefers to focus on social learning as it takes place in the home or in male-female relationships as explanations for domestic violence rather than examining the larger cultural context. Americans are exposed constantly to scenes of violence against women. In the movies or on television, women are shown being beaten, raped, or terrorized. Many researchers find credible evidence that these images convince at least some of the public that violence is acceptable (e.g., Malamuth & Check, 1981).

In the EDK poll, respondents were divided as to whether cultural representations influence behavior. Almost half (48%) agreed that these images do influence behavior, whereas the other half (50%) disagreed (see Table 3.5). About 20% strongly agreed with the statement, and a similar number strongly disagreed. Concern about cultural representation was strongest among white women (57% agreed) and African American women (47% agreed) and found least support among both Latinas and Latinos (37%).

Although the Latino respondents to the EDK poll did not think that television and movies promote violence, the focus group members strongly supported the argument that men who assault their wives are acting in response to cultural perceptions. They described violence as part of the macho culture. The Latinos felt there are still deep-rooted traditions of male dominance in society. Latinas noted a difference between men from Mexico and those born in the United States. They felt the former were more rigid, punitive, and domineering toward women. Many cited ignorance (lack of education) as the reason that men abused women.

Power Relationships

Some EDK study participants recognized that violence against women is not only about bad communication skills or early learning, it is also about power and control, the most widely accepted reasons for domestic violence cited by researchers and the reason most favored by advocates (Dobash & Dobash, 1992). Most respondents agreed that men who beat up their wives are using physical force to get their way (50% in total agreed with this statement, and 36% strongly agreed) (see Table 3.7). Women were more likely to agree strongly with the argument that battering was about power and control in relationships. White women expressed the strongest agreement (43% strongly agreed), perhaps reflecting a relatively greater influence of mainstream feminism among white females.

These views were reflected in the focus groups as well.

> He was frustrated because he couldn't control me, and he would make remarks about what I could do and what I couldn't do. He would treat me with disrespect.
>
> White woman (Hartford);
> college education or less

Some felt that men were increasingly threatened by feminism.

We have women's rights and they don't like it.

White woman (Hartford);
some college education or more

In the EDK survey, African Americans were more likely to see violence as an issue of power (30% strongly agreed). The opinions expressed in focus groups reflect this view that when a man hits a woman, he is trying to control her.

They look for someone they can intimidate. When I met my husband—we're not married now—we both were putting on our best behavior. He thought I was mild and meek. If you hit me, you're trying to hurt me. My father told me, "When a man hits you with his fist, make no mistake about it: he is trying to hurt you. It don't take that much to control a woman. You can take her, sit her in a chair, walk out of the room, you can go for a walk. Just walk away if it gets too much."

African American woman (Los Angeles);
high school graduate or some college education

I used to date a guy that, he would stand in front of the door and I couldn't get out. You might have to throw something at him, maybe, [laughs] to make him move. That's how he would show his masculine power or whatever, standing there, not letting me out.

African American woman (Dallas);
some college education

Whereas women in the EDK survey were more likely to agree strongly that violence is about power, the majority of men in all ethnic groups linked physical force with retaining control of women. This was most true for white men (28% strongly agreed with the statement and 55% agreed). A comment from the focus groups is typical:

My wife's ex-husband would take the coil wire off the car when he would go to work so that she couldn't go anywhere. That's what he would do to dominate. He would come in and emotionally and verbally abuse her, not only physically. He felt threatened and inferior to her.

White man (Dallas);
some college education or more

Latinos in the EDK survey also agreed with the statement that men use physical force to get their way (20% strongly agreed and 47% agreed), but in their conversations during focus groups, they focused on force as a means of compensating for the lack of other forms of power or sources of self-esteem.

The biggest problem with the violence and abuse, whether verbal or physical, is that men have a fear of losing their identity. If a person doesn't like himself, he is going to take it out on somebody else. . . . When our manhood is challenged by a woman's success, we have that inferiority complex where we are gonna take it out on somebody, somewhere. Fear causes anger. A guy just shot and killed his wife . . . the macho man that was going to control her by force. I go to him and talk to him and the next morning after he shot and killed his wife, and find him just whimpering.

> Latino (Los Angeles);
> some college education or less

Violence enters because you become accustomed to having things your own way. When things don't go your way, you want to push your weight. And women don't stand up to you, physically. They stand up to you by going out with someone else.

> Latino (Los Angeles);
> some college education or less

I think the decline for the man came about in the early sixties. That's when the women began to stand up for their rights. Began to get educated and they sort of have a tendency to stop being pushed around. Nowadays, it's hard to admit it, but there are very powerful women in the world and they are very well-educated.

> Latino (Los Angeles);
> married; high school graduate

In the EDK survey, Asian men also agreed that violence is an effort to control women (28% strongly agreed and 53% agreed). During focus groups, they said they believed that control is important and that men have a hard time learning how to exert it, especially when raising their daughters.

When raising a daughter, it is not always easy. A father is trying to teach his kids, girl or boy, the male's perspective about life, and sometime girls will not listen to the male's viewpoint. Thank God she found a man who could hopefully control her or tame her down. And you say, "Good luck, Charlie. Maybe you can teach her something about reality."

> Asian man (San Francisco);
> high school or college graduate

Old Excuses Don't Hold:
"He Was Drinking" or "She Asked for It"

As recently as 1968, 20% of American adults approved of "slapping one's spouse on appropriate occasions" (Stark & McEvoy, 1970, p. 52). In 1971, 62% of a primarily male sample of college students and middle-class businessmen felt that violence would "sometimes" be appropriate if the spouse was involved in an extramarital affair (Whitehurst, 1971). In the first (1978) University of New Hampshire national random survey, 27.6% of the couples felt that slapping a spouse was either necessary, normal, or good (Dibble & Straus, 1980).

As Greenblat (1985) noted, approval is very different from tolerance. Her 1983 survey of college students demonstrated that at that point in time, wife beating was severely disapproved of in the abstract, but that in "certain situations" (most notably sexual infidelity but also if the woman were physically abusing a child or screaming hysterically), it was tolerated (felt to be "OK") by the majority of male students and 40% of the females. Males were significantly more likely to express tolerance than were women under all conditions.

By 1992, significant gains had been made. The EDK survey suggested that the majority of the public no longer blamed the victim for incidents of violence or excused the abuser for his behavior. People rejected the age-old excuse of "He was drunk" as the reason that men beat women. In response to an open-ended question asking why a man would beat his wife, only 14% said he would do so because he was drunk and did not know what he was doing. In answer to a multiple-choice question on the same issue, 20% said a man would do so because he was drunk or got out of control. However, men (especially older men) were more likely than women to say he beat her because he was drunk or out of control (25% of men vs. 16% of women).

These results underscore the success of decades-long efforts by the movement against domestic violence to educate the public that "getting drunk" is not a reason for beating women. Despite a significant correlation between domestic violence and substance abuse across studies, most experts agree that the relationship is spurious (Fagan & Browne, 1994). Substance abuse is a problem for many batterers and one that needs intervention, but it is also clear from research and clinical experience that both problems need intervention, and substance abuse should never be seen as an excuse for battering. In fact, many of the focus group participants believed men use drinking as an excuse:

> There are men who beat without drinking. Men who drink and beat women, they drink in order to beat. They don't beat because they drink.
>
> > White woman (Hartford);
> > high school education or less

> I think they are looking for an excuse to punch her out, too. Like drinking would be "Oh, I had a couple of drinks, I didn't know I hit her." That's the most stupid excuse I ever heard of.
>
> > Asian woman (San Francisco);
> > high school or college graduate

They don't have to be a drinker to do it, but if they have that instinct and that feeling inside, that they want to have that power, then if they drink that just gives them the extra encouragement to do that sort of thing.

> White woman (Little Rock);
> high school education or less

However, the more recent Lieberman polls indicate that despite gains that have been made, this remains a difficult issue for people. When the question was phrased "men sometimes physically abuse women because they are *stressed out* or drunk," with the additional caveat, "it's not that they mean to hurt them," 38% of women and 55% of men respondents in November 1995 agreed. Because the question is confounded, it is hard to determine if the public has changed back toward seeing drinking as an excuse for battering or whether respondents are agreeing that men do not intend to hurt women. The public may very well be reluctant to ascribe to batterers an intent to harm, even if they do not agree that it is only a drinking problem. These inconsistencies highlight the difficulties we have, both as scientists and as citizens, in pinpointing why men beat women. There is probably no single answer, or different answers for different groups of men, and the public grasps this complexity.

Polling results also indicate that the movement to end domestic violence has been somewhat successful in leading people to stop blaming the victim. Only 12% of respondents to the original EDK survey agreed that a man would beat a woman because "she asked for it" by yelling and screaming at him (5%) or by cheating on him (7%). Some focus group participants said that women provoke men, but it was not a common argument. Although men did complain that women were abusive toward men, they did not condone a man beating a woman. Someone in every focus group said "He can always leave."

However, more recent results are puzzling and troublesome. In the November 1995 Lieberman poll, 38% of the sample (32% of women and 45% of men) agreed with the statement, "Some wives provoke their husbands into physically abusing them." Even though most respondents to that poll said they believe that domestic violence is an important social issue that must be addressed, about two out of five continued to hold opinions about domestic violence that can be construed as rationalizing it.

Whatever the Reason, It's Wrong

Whatever the reasons men beat women, all members of the focus groups recognized that this form of violence was more than just a physical assault. They strongly agreed that physical abuse robs women of self-confidence, hope, and self-esteem. They saw it as an attack on women's dignity and freedom, and they said there was no excuse for this violence. As stated earlier, one dominant theme emerged: *It doesn't matter why he beats her—it's wrong.*

I don't know [why her boyfriend beat her], but there's no reason to hit a woman. That's absolutely wrong. . . . If she did something horrible, you can leave.

> White man (Dallas);
> some college education or more

You never have justification for hitting.

> White man (Little Rock);
> college education or less

In many ways, group participants did not want to focus on the man who does the abusing. It seemed easier to keep him out of the conversation. They were much more comfortable talking about the woman—why she stays, what happens to her, and how they could help her. In a heartening sign of success for the battered women's movement, the participants expressed a great deal of sympathy and caring for abused women.

When a wom[a]n gets hit like that or abused, it does lower her self-esteem and self-confidence to that point where maybe they can't even get back up.

> White woman (Hartford);
> some college education

You keep telling somebody long enough [that it is their fault, that they are stupid or bad] and they are going to start believing it.

> African American man (Los Angeles);
> some college education or less

Almost everyone in the subsequent EDK poll agreed with the statement that violence against women is more than an assault, that it is an attack on women's dignity and freedom (see Table 3.7). Although most men and women strongly agreed with the statement, women were more likely to agree. There were significant gender differences among Caucasians (59% of women vs. 39% of men strongly agreed) and Latinos (43% of women compared with 24% of men strongly agreed). Among African Americans, men were significantly more likely than women to disagree with this statement (15% vs. 7%). Asian American males were more likely than their female counterparts to agree strongly with this statement (39% to 25%).

There were also differences across racial and ethnic groups in the EDK survey on this issue. White women were most likely to agree strongly that domestic violence is an attack on a woman's dignity and freedom (59% compared with 43% of Latinas, 38% of African American women, and 25% of Asian American women). Among men, Latinos were significantly less likely to agree strongly with the statement than were men from other racial and ethnic groups. There were no significant race or gender interactions based on either income or education.

The focus group conversations provided some evidence as to why some groups did not agree as strongly. White men agreed that a woman's self-esteem and confidence were robbed, but they resented the implication that this was men's motive for hitting them. Some African American women argued that a woman does not have to lose her self-esteem if she is battered. They talked about women in their mothers' generation who stayed with their partners because they had a strong sense of self-esteem and chose not to break up their families.

Latinas agreed that domestic violence robs women of their self-esteem, but they blamed the victim for letting the man do this to her. Similarly, several Latinos said the loss of a woman's confidence depends on her spirit. Asian women did not think most Asians focus on words like *self-esteem* and *self-confidence*.

Something Can Be Done

The good news is that 8 out of 10 respondents (81%) to the EDK survey believed that something can be done about the problem of domestic violence. Survey participants suggested that the best solution would be to provide support for the men to change individual behavior rather than punishing the crime or changing societal structures. Research supports that the latter two approaches are necessary for counseling to be effective (Dobash & Dobash, 1992; Sherman, 1992). Respondents looked more to counseling (22% of the total sample) and programs in school to teach children how to resolve conflicts (15%) as the primary solutions. Fewer people looked to punitive measures such as stronger laws (9%) or more arrests (5%).

Answers associated with the "family values" movement that has dominated the political debate in the past (as recently as the 1992 presidential campaign) did not seem relevant to the public's concerns as seen in the EDK data. Only a tiny percentage of respondents proposed the following "traditional" solutions: women should stay home (1%); people should go to church more (1%); or we should stop men from drinking (1%).

A portion of the EDK sample volunteered answers that echoed those expressed by feminists as well as the battered women's movement. About 17% of the total survey respondents suggested the following feminist solutions: helping women become less emotionally and economically dependent upon men (7%); reducing violence in the media (4%); and generally changing society (6%).

TABLE 3.7 Percentage of Respondents Who Held Beliefs About Causes of Domestic Violence, by Race and Gender

	Caucasian		African American				Asian American	
	Women (n = 395)	Men (n = 388)	Women (n = 154)	Men (n = 150)	Latinas (n = 150)	Latinos (n = 152)	Women (n = 156)	Men (n = 161)
Beating up on women is often learned in the home. Some people learn to be violent because when they were young, they were beaten, or witnessed violence in their home.								
Strongly agree	57[a]	44	35[b]	33	41[b]	27	36	40
Agree	36	42	48	40	40	53	48	46
Disagree	3	7	12	14	18	17	17	13
Men who beat women do it to humiliate and bully them.								
Strongly agree	34[b]	21	25[b]	17	20[b]	16	22[c]	24
Agree	47	46	45	46	41	45	38	51
Disagree	11	24	18	23	33	28	30	24
People may say it is wrong to hit women, but the constant pictures of women getting beaten, raped, or terrorized on television and in movies says that this violence is acceptable.								
Strongly agree	27[b]	17	13[b]	15	14[b]	12	13	13
Agree	30	23	34	27	23	24	27	27
Disagree	21	36	30	37	43	47	60	60
As long as women are economically dependent on men, they will be potential victims of violence.								
Strongly agree	29[b]	15	21[b]	20	31[b]	22	13	12
Agree	38	41	36	31	37	30	34	44
Disagree	22	28	32	34	23	41	52	43
As long as women are emotionally dependent on men, they will be potential victims of violence.								
Strongly agree	31[b]	18	22[b]	22	35[b]	25	16	13
Agree	45	47	50	37	34	38	37	44
Disagree	15	23	18	27	22	28	46	43

Personal Accountability

Even in 1992, Americans had a sense that domestic violence is not a problem that should be left for someone else to solve. Among EDK poll respondents, and across genders and ethnic groups, there appeared to be a strong sense of personal accountability relating to ending physical abuse (see Table 3.8). Almost all

TABLE 3.7 *Continued*

	Caucasian		African American				Asian American	
	Women (n = 395)	Men (n = 388)	Women (n = 154)	Men (n = 150)	Latinas (n = 150)	Latinos (n = 152)	Women (n = 156)	Men (n = 161)
Violence against women is more than a physical assault. It is an attack on a woman's dignity and freedom.								
Strongly agree	59[d]	39	38[b]	35	43[b]	24	25[a]	39
Agree	37	48	48	43	46	51	57	53
Disagree	2	11	7	12	6	19	18	
Men who beat up their wives are using physical force to get their way.								
Strongly agree	43[b]	29	30[b]	29	37[b]	20	27[e]	30
Agree	45	55	53	45	45	47	48	58
Disagree	10	14	10	17	13	27	25	13

SOURCE: These data are from a 1992 poll conducted by EDK Associates, working with the Family Violence Prevention Fund. For details see Appendix B.

NOTE: The following p values are for gender differences within racial groups. Where no p value is given, any differences are nonsignificant.

a. $p = .02$.

b. $p = .00$.

c. $p = .03$.

d. $p = .06$.

e. $p = .04$.

responded that they would talk to friends, family, or clergy to figure out how to help someone they knew who was being beaten (93%). More women than men (93% compared with 86%) said they would call the police if they witnessed a man beating a woman. Most said they would intervene if they knew the offender, telling him to stop (79%). However, a significantly larger (83% vs. 75%) proportion of men than women said they would tell the person to stop. The lower percentage for women may reflect their concerns for personal safety upon "confrontation" (discussed in more depth in Chapter 6).

Even in 1992, when less public attention was being paid to the issue, Americans supported public funding and collective efforts to reduce violence against women. Almost 9 in 10 respondents to the EDK survey said they would support legislation to increase funding for battered women's programs (87%), and 2 out of 3 said they would personally give money to an organization working on this issue (69%). Many said they would even give their time (57% of women and 39% of men). Significantly more women than men supported all three of these responses.

TABLE 3.8   Percentage of Respondents Who Said They Would Personally Take Action to Help Reduce Violence Against Women

	All	*Women*	*Men*
If you knew someone who was being beaten, would you talk to your friends, family, or clergy to try to figure out how to help this person?	93	93	92
Would you tell the person to stop?	79	75	83
Would you call the police if you saw a man beating his wife or girlfriend?	90	93	86
Would you support legislation to increase funding for battered women's programs?	87	91	84
Would you give money to an organization working on this issue?	69	73	64
Would you volunteer some time and work in a program for battered women?	48	57	39

SOURCE: These data are from a 1992 poll conducted by EDK Associates, working with the Family Violence Prevention Fund. For details see Appendix B.

Data collected by Lieberman Research only 2 years later (July 1994) indicates, however, that *actual* public engagement in efforts to end domestic violence remains quite low compared with other social change efforts that have been popularized over the years—only 18% of the total sample had done *anything at all* about the problem, including talking with a woman they knew who was being battered. The EDK results, then, indicate not what people were actually willing to do about domestic violence in 1992, but rather a sense of concern about it. Even at that time, most respondents clearly did not consider it socially acceptable to say they would "ignore" the problem. Actually getting involved, however, is another story. Successes on that front, as well as strategies for involving the public in this problem, are discussed at length in Chapter 6.

Summary

Our survey and focus group participants were somewhat uncomfortable with attributing causation for domestic violence. A large percentage stated that they didn't know why men would abuse their female intimate partners. This response reflects the state of the science about domestic violence, as well as people's genuine confusion about why men who say they love a woman would hit or otherwise abuse her. The research evidence is mixed regarding which causative factors respondents agreed with most strongly. All the causes mentioned garnered at least some agreement. Respondents were reluctant to attribute to men premeditated, "on purpose" motivations to hurt their female partners physically or psychologically, in spite of research evidence that a small but significant proportion of batterers are probably psychopaths (Dutton, 1988). However, the overwhelming majority of our sample recognized the controlling aspects involved in domestic violence, and few were willing to excuse the batterers' behavior totally. The implications of these findings suggest that public educators and advocates would do best to avoid discussing hypothetical causes of domestic violence, but rather to echo the public's sentiment that violence is just plain wrong, no matter what the reason, and that it must not be tolerated.

Drawing the Line

Before people and communities will be spurred to take action against domestic violence, they must decide that a line has been crossed that merits it. Most Americans tolerate a fair amount of abusive behavior by men against their female intimate partners, still considering it a private matter. Where do people draw the line? When does a private fight become a matter of community concern? Of public policy? Our research yields some answers.

Drawing the Line

According to the 1992 EDK survey, a fight was perceived to become a matter of public policy when it involved injury (see Table 4.1). Most men and women across all racial/ethnic groups felt it was none of their business if a man and woman were having a fight and he screamed at her or said abusive things.

On the other hand, the majority of respondents to the EDK poll (and the majority of each racial and ethnic group) agreed that when a man threatens a woman, the fight becomes a public matter. There were, however, significant racial/ethnic differences. Caucasians were most likely to identify threats as a public matter (67%), whereas Latinos (51%) were least likely to make this assessment.

Perhaps Americans' perception of the seriousness of threats stems from their understanding that the key defining characteristic of domestic violence is fear. One focus group respondent said,

If you are afraid, then whether it is a tickle or a smack, it's abusive. If you are afraid that you are going to be hurt, that's abuse.

> White woman (Hartford);
> high school education or less

But although threats may create a context for social intervention, survey respondents supported private rather than public intervention in cases involving this kind of behavior. For instance, only one out of three people in the EDK survey wanted a husband arrested for threatening his wife, and few would encourage the victim to leave him in such a situation. Among those who agreed that threats are a form of domestic violence, less than half wanted the man arrested or the woman to leave. There were sex differences among Caucasians and African Americans, with women significantly more likely than men to say she should leave. Among Asian Americans, men were even more likely than women to say it becomes someone else's business when a man threatens a woman.

For most, the line between a fight and domestic violence had less to do with the psychological element of fear than it did with physical injury. Even at the point of physical contact, when respondents were told that the man "grabs and shoves" the woman, *only one half of each race and ethnic group thought this behavior merited the man being arrested.*

Indeed, there was no consensus on his being arrested, even among those who were clear that his grabbing and shoving her constituted domestic violence. There was also little encouragement for her to leave the relationship. However, Caucasian respondents to the EDK poll were significantly more likely than other groups to favor the victim leaving under these circumstances. Among African Americans, women were more likely than men to favor her leaving him (62% to 48%).

There was a degree of physical violence in male-female relationships that most people didn't seem to think was right, but for which they would nevertheless not call on the police for help. Respondents to the EDK survey considered forms of violence such as pushing, slapping, or grabbing worthy of condemnation, and they wanted these types of abuse stopped. Again, however, many would not put a man in jail for these acts, and only a handful believed the woman should leave the man in these circumstances. In situations in which abuse did not result in serious injury to the woman, respondents thought the best solution would be to recommend counseling, with a focus on improving communication skills.

Some participants in the focus groups believed that men who slap, push, or shove can change. Several women participants described husbands who in the past had grabbed them and hurt them when they lost their temper—and then "straightened out."

TABLE 4.1 When Does a Fight Become a Public Issue? Responses by Race and
Gender

	Percentage of Respondents Who Believe:		
	It's a Public Issue	He Should Be Arrested	She Should Leave Him
When he screams abusive things			
Caucasian women	17	1[a]	8
Caucasian men	14	2	5
African American women	30	9	12
African American men	19	6	9
Latinas	18	3	6
Latinos	14	3	3
Asian American women	26	32	16
Asian American men	19	23	24
When he threatens her			
Caucasian women	69	22	39[b]
Caucasian men	63	17	28
African American women	60	33	31
African American men	57	29	21
Latinas	52	24	21
Latinos	42	22	16
Asian American women	54[a]	47	33
Asian American men	67	39	57
When he grabs and shoves her			
Caucasian women	72	35[c]	44
Caucasian men	71	29	38
African American women	60	33	36[d]
African American men	59	25	28
Latinas	65	35	28
Latinos	57	26	20
Asian American women	65	49	34[e]
Asian American men	61	56	58

> I said I would never let anyone be physical with me and I've never been beaten.
> But I have been grabbed and pushed. I said I would never accept a man showing
> me enough anger to even think to grab and push me. . . . I said we cannot have
> this. I cannot live like this. I will not be intimidated. [Moderator: And what
> happened?] We talked and he's not put his hands on me ever again.
>
> African American woman (Los Angeles);
> high school graduate or some college education

Many men admitted that their first marriages had failed because they did not
know how to communicate constructively or control their anger. They felt

TABLE 4.1 *Continued*

	Percentage of Respondents Who Believe:		
	It's a Public Issue	*He Should Be Arrested*	*She Should Leave Him*
When he slaps her hard			
Caucasian women	86	52	61[e]
Caucasian men	88	51	54
African American women	66	47	46
African American men	62	39	39
Latinas	78	56[c]	46
Latinos	74	49	43
Asian American women	77	58	51
Asian American men	77	69	55
When he punches her			
Caucasian women	94	83[f]	81[f]
Caucasian men	96	77	73
African American women	75	64	53
African American men	69	57	62
Latinas	91	85	69
Latinos	84	78	62
Asian American women	88	82	66[d]
Asian American men	88	84	86

SOURCE: These data are from a 1992 poll conducted by EDK Associates, working with the Family Violence Prevention Fund. For details see Appendix B.

NOTE: The following p values are for gender differences within racial groups. Where no p value is given, any differences are nonsignificant.

a. $p = .01$.

b. $p = .03$.

c. $p = .04$.

d. $p = .05$.

e. $p = .02$.

f. $p = .005$.

that they had since learned how to do so and did not think of themselves as abusers.

> I didn't . . . knock her with my fist. I just slapped her down. Then she shut up. We both made each other mad. We just pushed each other's buttons like crazy, and we just didn't have any tools that are available nowadays for people to get along better. There's a lot of wonderful things that I've gotten into since then that I wish I'd have known back when I was married.
>
> White man (Dallas);
> some college education or more

The Line Is Drawn at Physical Injury

At the outset of our work, physical, visible injury or threat of injury was where the public drew the line to divide abusive behavior from domestic violence. In the 1992 EDK survey, 86% of respondents said that when a man hits a woman hard, his actions should no longer be a private matter. Slightly more than half of respondents were ready to insist on societal sanctions at that point, agreeing that he should be arrested (53%) or she should leave him (53%). Similarly, the EDK poll showed that there was absolutely no doubt that a man had "crossed the line" if he punched a woman. Nine out of ten (94%) respondents said that this was a public matter. Most people wanted to see the man arrested for this behavior (80%), and they wanted the victim to leave him (76%).

Class factors did not influence people's response regarding when a fight became other people's business. Education and income had almost no influence on how men and women of each ethnic group in the EDK poll responded to this question. Interaction effects of class (measured by education and income separately) with ethnicity and gender were examined by analyses of variance (ANOVA) without any significant findings, except the proportion expected by chance (15 of 288 analyses).

The more recent Lieberman polls reinforce these findings. In the November 1995 poll, 82% of the sample, across all demographic groups, believed that other people should get involved if a husband hits his wife, even if she is not injured. But if she were injured to the extent that she required medical attention, 96% said that other people should get involved.

Defining Domestic Violence

To help clarify the public's definition of domestic violence, EDK survey respondents were presented with a series of vignettes identified as common situations: a woman screaming at or hitting her child at a mall; neighbors fighting; a fight at a family holiday meal; and a fight between a husband and wife. They were then asked to assess whether the described circumstances constituted domestic violence and whether the man should be arrested and the woman encouraged to leave. These vignettes compared similar circumstances involving different degrees of physical violence. We found that people supported public intervention (e.g., arrest for him or help for her to leave) only in cases in which injury was explicit in the description (see Table 4.2).

The majority of EDK respondents felt that a mother screaming at her child was child abuse. If their daughter's husband grabbed her and called her a worthless cow or their neighbors were fighting and screaming at the top of their lungs, they believed that these situations constituted domestic violence. However, in all three of these scenarios, respondents were not willing to impose strong sanctions. Only a few said they would remove the child from the home (6%), and a small percentage would seek arrest for the screaming neighbor (10%) or the abusive husband (15%); few men and women would tell their neighbor to leave her husband (15%) and less than half (41%) thought their daughter should leave the husband.

Once the EDK poll scenarios involved clear injury, such as the mother smacking the child hard across the face and head or the husband or boyfriend punching their daughter in the face, then respondents stated that they would want the child removed from the home (40%) and the man arrested (69%). They also would want the woman to leave the man (72%).

Another series of EDK vignettes compared similar circumstances involving different degrees of physical violence. For example, in the first case, the daughter calls and reports that her husband or boyfriend grabbed her by the blouse and called her a worthless cow. In the second case, the daughter reports that he called her a tramp and punched her in the face.

The majority of EDK respondents in each race and gender group said that the first example was a case of domestic violence. Once again, white men were least likely to label this incident as domestic violence (55%), and Latinas and African American women were most likely to use this label (73%). However, calling it domestic violence did not translate into support for intervention among respondents. Less than a third of any group felt that the man should be arrested for this kind of behavior, and only 40% would encourage the woman to leave. In the case of the man punching the woman, the overwhelming majority of every racial and ethnic group defined it as domestic violence and wanted him arrested and her to leave (see Table 4.1).

Is the Line Moving?

The most recent polls conducted by Lieberman Research herald some exciting news for battered women's advocates who have been working diligently for so many years to educate the public about the serious nature of different forms of abuse. It appears that Americans are more willing now than they were a couple of years ago to seek outside intervention for domestic violence situations that do not involve physical injury to women.

To assess people's tolerance for various forms of domestic violence and the perceived appropriateness of outside intervention for each, respondents to the Lieberman polls were read several descriptions of different types of domestic disputes that hypothetically occur in a couple's home. After hearing each description, respondents were asked if they would consider the dispute a private affair between the couple or whether they believed it required other people to

TABLE 4.2 Reactions to Conflict Situations Between Men and Women,
by Race and Gender

	Percentage of Respondents Who Believe:		
	This Is Domestic Violence	He Should Be Arrested	She Should Leave Him
Suppose your neighbors were having another fight screaming at each other at the top of their lungs.			
White women	58	13	18
White men	50	7	12
African American women	63	27	21
African American men	61	23	17
Latinas	59	21	14
Latinos	45	12	12
Asian American women	41	15	19
Asian American men	44	19	17
Suppose your neighbors were having a huge fight and you knew she was being beaten.			
White women	98	78	68
White men	98	71	54
African American women	85	72	59
African American men	84	65	51
Latinas	93	87	61
Latinos	91	78	49
Asian American women	91	65	47
Asian American men	94	78	64
You are at a large family dinner and your cousin is fighting with his wife. He shoves her and smacks her across the face.			
White women	91	31	42
White men	91	24	30
African American women	81	52	40
African American men	73	35	33
Latinas	87	49	33
Latinos	78	35	21
Asian American women	79	22	30
Asian American men	79	30	31

get involved. As of November 1995, an overwhelming majority of respondents (96%) continued to believe that outside intervention is required in a situation in which a man physically abuses his wife and causes injuries that require medical attention. What's more, a significant majority also want outside intervention if he hits his wife but she isn't injured (82%) (see Table 4.3).

TABLE 4.2 Reactions to Conflict Situations Between Men and Women,
by Race and Gender

	Percentage of Respondents Who Believe:		
	This Is Domestic Violence	*He Should Be Arrested*	*She Should Leave Him*
Your daughter calls you after she and her husband or boyfriend had a big fight where he grabbed her by the blouse and called her a worthless cow.			
White women	63	15	44
White men	55	13	35
African American women	72	29	42
African American men	68	29	41
Latinas	73	27	49
Latinos	64	24	38
Asian American women	58	19	45
Asian American men	62	20	43
Your daughter calls you after she and her husband or boyfriend get into a big fight where he called her a tramp and punched her in the face.			
White women	97	72	78
White men	95	66	68
African American women	89	69	69
African American men	86	69	69
Latinas	93	81	67
Latinos	95	71	67
Asian American women	87	59	64
Asian American men	90	71	74

SOURCE: These data are from a 1992 poll conducted by EDK Associates, working with the Family Violence Prevention Fund. For details see Appendix B.

In addition, there have been significant gains in recent years in public intolerance for forms of abuse that do not involve physical contact. For example, whereas only 19% of respondents in November 1995 supported outside intervention if a husband insults his wife, that number was up from only 12% in the Lieberman poll taken a year earlier, between November 1994 and February 1995. And whereas the November 1995 poll indicates that one out of every four respondents (24%) support outside intervention when a husband shouts curses at his wife and pounds his fist on the table, only one in five (19%) did so a year earlier. These results are exciting changes for battered women's advocates, who know that earlier intervention isn't just a theoretical issue—it can actually save lives.

TABLE 4.3 Percentage of Respondents Who Believe Domestic Disputes Require
Outside Intervention: Changes Over Time

	July 1994 (N = 735)	January-February 1995[a] (N = 486)	November 1995 (N = 742)	January-February 1995 Versus November 1995
A husband . . .				
Insults his wife	10	12	19	+7
Shouts curses at his wife and pounds his fist on the table	19	28	24	−4
Hits his wife but she isn't injured	80	87	82	−5[b]
Physically abuses his wife and causes injuries that require medical attention	97	99	96	−3[b]

SOURCE: These data are from polls conducted by Lieberman Research, Inc., working with the Family
Violence Prevention Fund and The Advertising Council. For details see Appendix C.

a. The second wave of polling by Lieberman Research took place from November 1994 to February 1995.
However, data from the shorter January-February period were used here so that they would be more
comparable to the first- and third-wave polls, which were conducted in a single month.

b. Differences significant at a 95% confidence interval.

Survey Results in the Context of Other Evidence

A random sample telephone survey was conducted in Marin County, California,
an upper middle-class community adjacent to San Francisco (Marin Abused
Women's Services, 1993). The study comprised 402 white men; most (79%)
were between 25 and 64 years old, and 82% had some college education or more.
In response to hypothetical scenarios, 63% said they would intervene if a friend
was constantly making fun of his girlfriend, 70% if he was continually criticizing
her—and 93% if he grabbed her and wouldn't let go. The results of this study,
although based on only one small geographical region of the United States,
corroborate the findings of the national polling by EDK and Lieberman Research
reported here.

The actions that the public endorses in response to serious violence will be
effective only if: community supports, employment opportunities, and continued protection are provided by the criminal justice system and neighbors to help
battered women to leave; the total community context enforces batterers'
completing long-term treatment; and severe community sanctions are consistently and rigorously imposed against offenders (Pence & Shepard, 1988;
Sullivan, Campbell, Angelique, Eby, & Davidson, 1994). Research shows
significant changes in public perception, but further transformation is needed
not only toward intolerance but toward personal responsibility for action.

Summary

EDK Polling results indicate that whereas Americans perceive a great deal of abusive behavior between men and women as wrong, they believe that domestic violence becomes a matter requiring public intervention only at the point when injury occurs. In these findings, there were more similarities than differences across demographic groupings of gender, ethnicity, education, and income. Where there were differences, gender was consistently the most frequently disparate, with ethnicity second. Men across ethnic and social groups were less likely than women to label examples of coercive behavior as abusive and less likely to recommend strong action against such behavior. The gender differences were present within each of the ethnic groups and are discussed more fully in Chapter 5, along with differences between ethnic groups. In an encouraging sign of progress, the Lieberman poll in November 1995 indicates that while an overwhelming consensus remains for intervention at the point of physical injury, the public may have become less tolerant of other forms of abuse and more willing to intervene before injury has occurred. Implications of this research for public education and mobilization efforts are discussed in the final chapter.

"Water on Rock"

Changing Domestic Violence Perceptions in the African American, Asian American, and Latino Communities

Doris Williams Campbell, Beckie Masaki, and Sara Torres

> At first appearance, a boulder seems strong and water seems weak. Yet drop by drop, water can break down a boulder. Drop by drop, we can turn the tide.

Domestic violence is a serious and pervasive problem in all three ethnic populations discussed in this chapter, and in every community in the United States. Each of the three communities is different, with varying cultural norms related to domestic violence and varying perceptions about its occurrence. Without an understanding of the specific norms and perceptions, efforts to change community perceptions and decrease violence cannot succeed.

Effective strategies in all communities of color must address the values in transition in those communities—historical perspectives (traditional as well as "cultures of resistance"), the impact of racism, anti-immigrant sentiment, and the cultural "freeze"—and develop strategies that include leadership from within the communities themselves.

Despite the challenges, the specific ethnic communities that are our focus have strengths, such as well-developed, intact community structures and bicultural perspectives. These strengths represent tremendous potential for developing innovative, successful community responses toward ending domestic violence. A national strategy that incorporates ethnic-specific approaches can create the diversity necessary to resonate among all Americans and reinforce the message that there is no excuse for domestic violence.

It is important to remember that different ethnic groups receive different societal opportunities and rewards and share different attitudes and goals (Lystad, 1986). An individual's ethnic heritage influences his or her attitudes, values, personality, and behavior. Although America comprises many ethnic groups, cultural norms emphasize an assimilationist model—conformity toward an Anglo ideology. Services for ethnic groups are simultaneously judged and categorized in accordance with a rigidly adhered-to, mainstream, white value orientation. The "melting pot" theory notwithstanding, ethnic and cultural diversity remains a reality and must be addressed at all levels because it epitomizes "the very fabric of American society" (Cafferty & Chestang, 1976, p. xi).

In the area of domestic violence, cultural factors must be considered at all levels if battered women are to be served effectively and sensitively. The majority of the literature to date on wife abuse states that cross-cultural differences do not exist among families experiencing wife abuse. Research regarding cross-cultural differences is scant. This chapter will present what is known about domestic violence in each of our three ethnic communities, integrating the research findings from the EDK survey and focus groups with pragmatic realities and personal understandings. As advocates and practitioners for and with battered women, as well as members of our own ethnic communities, we will present in this chapter our own experiences as we interpret the data. The chapter will also explore some of the issues related to conducting research on wife abuse in communities of color.

The terms *African American* and *black* are used interchangeably, acknowledging that all blacks in the United States (Haitians, black Cubans, Jamaicans, and so on) share roots originating in Africa. The terminology of *Latino* couples and *Latina* women is used to refer to Mexican American, Puerto Rican, Cuban American, and other Central American groups, except where other researchers have used the term *Hispanic*. Throughout the chapter, the term *Asian* is used to describe the broad range of people with ancestral heritage in the continent of Asia and the Pacific Islands. The term *Asian American* is used to describe Asian people living in the United States, including immigrants, refugees, and those born in the United States.

Stereotypes

Stereotypes about all three ethnic groups intersect with the public perception of domestic violence in our communities and with the attitudes of individual people regarding men beating women, for example, stereotypes about Asian Americans as the "model minority," with no social problems; about Latinos as illegal "aliens"; and about African Americans as being more violent than other groups. These stereotypes contribute to the general public's willingness to see the groups as "the Other" and therefore more likely to have problems with domestic violence. Misconceptions and racist attitudes about violence and people of color contribute to their reluctance to discuss domestic violence publicly. The complicated dynamic of changing cultural values in a multicultural society, the diverse range of people incorporated into the terms *Asian American, African American,* and *Latino* or *Hispanic,* as well as the lack of resources to meet the particular needs of battered women of color, are only a few of the factors that create a challenge in efforts to change public perceptions of domestic violence in ethnic communities.

Research on Domestic Violence Related to Ethnicity

Research on domestic violence has emerged only during the past two decades. Until recently, the experiences of nonmajority women were absent from much of the mainstream literature on domestic violence (Asbury, 1987). Omission of race/ethnicity in the mainstream abuse research typically occurs by:

1. Omitting the description of the race or ethnicity of the women studied
2. Including only majority women
3. Including nonrepresentative proportions of nonmajority groups
4. Including representative proportions of minority groups in an overall sample size too small for appropriate comparisons
5. Failing to analyze the results according to ethnicity

In examining the literature on violence in minority communities, several other problematic issues arise that make it difficult to compare data across studies. First, the indicators used to determine the incidence of family violence differ greatly. Also, many of the large surveys are collected through self-report telephone interviews. Because of the disproportionate level of poverty in Latino, African American, and immigrant Asian American groups, these people are less likely to have telephones. Another issue is language for Latino and Asian American immigrant populations. Many people needed to have the interview questions translated into the multiple dialects of each major language. In addition, the validity of translations becomes a research factor. Other than a few population-based surveys, most studies of domestic violence are based on small, nonrepresentative shelter or clinical samples, and few researchers have studied domestic violence issues unique to women of color from any ethnic group

(Asbury, 1987). A full range of studies is needed to understand fully domestic violence in communities of color, comparative and within group, population based and clinical, and survey and in-depth. The research reported here contributes to the literature by including women of color from each of the three major ethnic groups in the design of the research surveys and focus groups; women of color were also participants in data collection and contributors to the interpretation of the cultural content and context of the findings.

Two national random surveys of domestic violence conducted by Straus and Gelles (1975 with a follow-up in 1985, see Straus & Gelles, 1990) provided data that can be used to make comparisons of rates of domestic violence across racial/ethnic groups. Results of the 1975 National Family Violence Survey (Straus et al., 1980), until recently cited as the primary source of data on the prevalence of spousal violence among African Americans, reported that wife abuse was nearly four times higher among black couples than among white couples. This finding reinforced prevailing stereotypes about black men being more violent in their heterosexual relationships than white men. Among the limitations of this survey were the small sample of African American families (n = 147) and a limited sampling frame (Hampton & Coner-Edwards, 1993). This survey, like the majority of other general violence studies, failed to consider social class or income in calculating violence rates (even though these are problematic as indicators of socioeconomic status). It did not consider that socioeconomic differences between the races rather than race itself may explain the discrepant rates. A reanalysis of the 1980 results (Hampton, Gelles, & Harrop, 1989; Straus & Gelles, 1990) found that controlling for socioeconomic status (SES) resulted in a lower differential rate of husband to wife violence between black and white couples. Cazenave and Straus (1979) also analyzed these initial data and found that lower levels of spousal violence in African American couples were associated with embeddedness in primary networks, number of years in the neighborhood, the number of children, and the number of nonnuclear family members in the household. The analyses revealed the importance of studying variations in rates of violence among ethnic groups according to family income, social class, and strength of social networks.

Studies designed to evaluate specifically the convergence of race and class in explaining domestic violence rates (Lockhart, 1985, 1991; Lockhart & White, 1989) demonstrated virtually no differences in the prevalence of wife abuse among African American and European American women of varying social classes. Lockhart found that a larger proportion of middle-class African American women than of middle-class white women reported violent treatment at the hand of their partners. However, the median rate of violent episodes experienced by middle-class white women was somewhat higher than that for middle-class black women. Arguing that African American couples are not inherently more violent than white couples, Lockhart asserted that when higher levels of violence exist, they may be due in part to the particular social predicament of African Americans in American society, including aggressive and violent problem-solving strategies retained from their lower-SES developmental experiences, because for many African Americans, middle-class status is a relatively recent achievement. Using education as the most salient proxy for SES across ethnic groups, the current research found no statistically significant relationships concerning the prevalence of male violence toward females.

The second National Family Violence Survey provided comparative data on rates of couple violence for African Americans, non-Hispanic whites, and Hispanics (Straus & Gelles, 1986). It improved on the first survey by oversampling within two major ethnic groups, African Americans and Hispanics. However, the survey combined all the Latino ethnic groups together as "Hispanic" without identifying what proportions of each were represented. The results of this survey indicated that whatever forces led to an overall decrease in reported violence toward women from 1975 to 1985 benefited minority women to a greater degree than majority women. The 1985 results revealed that black and Hispanic families had comparable rates of husband-to-wife violence and that both groups had a rate of severe assaults on wives more than double the rate in non-Hispanic white families. Regarding wife-to-husband violence, white women had the lowest rates (115 per 1,000), black women (207 per 1,000) had the highest rates, and the rates for Hispanic females fell in the middle. African American women also had the highest rates of severe violence, followed by Hispanic women, then white women. Although income inequalities are a factor in explaining differences in rates of violence between African American and white families, controlling for income does not account totally for the racial disparity. Additional factors must be considered in assessing domestic violence among African American (and other ethnic minority) couples (Hampton & Gelles, 1993).

In contrast to the National Family Violence Surveys, data from the National Victim Survey found no significant differences among the three largest ethnic groups (Anglo American, African American, and Hispanic) in rates of serious violence (serious enough to be considered a crime) from intimates (Bachman, 1994). Differences in how the questions were asked across the three surveys likely contributed to the differences in findings.

Studies are needed to determine how much variance in domestic violence among any ethnic group and across ethnic groups is explained by other relevant variables while controlling for SES across all levels. These variables include such structural stressors and contextual factors as joblessness, poverty, lack of education, and living in rural versus urban environments. When such studies are conducted, it is imperative that the measurement instruments are accurate and appropriate for use with different ethnic and cultural groups and that questionnaires and items on instruments are consistently interpreted within and across ethnic and cultural groups. D. W. Campbell and colleagues (1994) found that one measure of spouse abuse, the Index of Spouse Abuse (ISA), revealed a different factor structure when used with African American women than was found with the original ISA subscale. This study demonstrated the critical need to evaluate the extent to which instruments developed to measure spouse or partner abuse are valid and reliable when used with diverse groups that may not have been represented in the samples used for initial instrument development and validation.

An Ecological Framework

Family violence and the high rates of family violence among minorities may be examined using the ecological approach, which views the family as an interactive system vis-à-vis the external environment. Some of the factors that put families at risk for wife abuse are the factors minority families experience every day as a result of their position in American society.

One risk factor is external stress. Investigators have found a positive relationship between external stress and child abuse and wife abuse. Gelles and Straus (1988) noted that families that have less education and lower occupational status were more likely to experience stress and less likely to have the resources to cope with that stress. These families generally experienced more family violence. The living conditions, as well as majority group discrimination against minority groups in the United States, create a great deal of stress. Another risk factor is social isolation. Again, research has shown that families that are socially isolated from friends and other family members tended to have higher rates of wife abuse and different kinds of family violence. Thus a person with friends or relatives living nearby was found to be less likely to be involved in an abusive relationship. For immigrant groups where family is extremely important culturally, social isolation is a significant problem.

Poverty is another factor contributing to wife abuse. One of the structural theories associated with murders and family violence posits that the stresses under which poor families live might cause more violence. Some 40% of Latino families live in poverty, according to the 1990 U.S. Census. Discrimination, poverty, substance abuse, and violence all interact in complex ways, each reinforcing the other and placing ethnic minority groups at increased risk for domestic violence without ethnicity necessarily being a risk factor in and of itself. Structural realities are at least as important as cultural norms.

In a different focus group analysis, Campbell, Pugh, Campbell, and Visscher (1995) talked with two ethnically heterogeneous (African American, European American, Native American, and Latina) groups of battered women. The values and attitudes about controlling women and appropriate "manhood" held by their partners, which the women had attributed to their specific culture, actually turned out to be remarkably similar across ethnic groups. Sorenson (1996) noted the same phenomenon in her excellent focus group (African American, Anglo, Mexican American, and Korean American) analysis of the need for inclusion of the influence of the intersection of ethnicity and gender in domestic violence research, policy, and service provision.

Impact of Racism and Anti-immigrant Sentiment

The experience of being a minority group member in the United States is qualitatively different from that of being a member of the dominant culture (Asbury, 1993). The experience and effects of racism are daily, insidious, interactive, and incalculable. Immigrant women are members of all three of the ethnic groups discussed here, and immigrants as well as those born in the United States face racism, anti-immigrant sentiment, and a dominant culture that is unfamiliar and sometimes in direct conflict with the cultural values of their countries of origin. Immigrant battered women and their children suffer the same barriers as all domestic violence survivors, but they face additional barriers if they do not speak English, do not know the law or their rights, lack job and educational opportunities, and lack access to language- and culture-competent services. Their immigrant status is an additional source of stress. If the woman is in this country illegally, she may be afraid to seek help. Also, immigrant women may have left family and friends, their major sources of psychological and financial support.

Male batterers use race, culture, and immigration status to control their partners. Batterers frequently accuse their partners of "becoming too American-ized," "betraying their culture, family, and community," and "not being a good Filipina/Japanese/Korean/Mexican/Cuban/Puerto Rican/Guatemalan/Haitian— and so on—woman." Other controlling behavior includes males "forbidding" female partners to learn English, access public transportation, or acquire independent skills necessary to negotiate life in a new country. Immigrant battered women who are dependent on U.S.-citizen spouses for their immigration status are often threatened with deportation by the batterer. Whether threats regarding immigration status are real or perceived by the batterer, a battered woman often has no access to accurate information about her rights. Anti-immigrant legislation and general sentiment in the United States feed into a dynamic of reduced access to alternatives and a rising sense of hopelessness for immigrant battered women. Batterers will attempt to excuse their abusive behavior as "culturally acceptable" or as a consequence of racism, immigrant stresses, or other forms of victimization.

Domestic violence crosses all lines, but services and responses designed to address the needs of battered women do not reach all segments of the population.

The severe lack of services and information for and/or specific to battered women from marginalized communities renders the women extremely vulnerable. Without alternatives, battered women of color are not safe to speak out or escape violent relationships. Racism, anti-immigrant sentiment, and strategies that do not match the needs of women of particular ethnic groups create an environment that effectively silences battered women and obstructs the potential for change in public perceptions of domestic violence in those communities.

Asian American and other immigrant cultures commonly respond to the dominant culture by clinging to the traditions and identity of their homeland. Retaining cultural traditions and identity contribute to a healthy society that is rich in diversity, but when outmoded traditions such as domestic violence are rigidly clung to, in what is known as a "cultural freeze," the consequences destroy family and community. Negotiating life with multiple cultural values, all of which are in continual evolution, is confusing. We must begin to draw global connections to paint a more complete picture of the changing status of women around the world, incorporating the history and the currently growing worldwide movements against domestic violence. Without a global connection, Asian Americans and other communities of color can too easily dismiss public messages against domestic violence as exclusive, or as emphasizing a Western or American anti-male concept with no connection to Eastern, African, or Latino values.

Domestic Violence in the African American Community

Some scholars write that the historical literature fails to find any evidence of ill treatment of African women by their male partners. During the entire reign of the pharaohs in Egypt, African women purportedly enjoyed complete freedom, in contrast to the condition of segregation experienced by European women of ancient and medieval times. If these accounts are true, the pattern of spouse abuse as reported in the recent literature (where African American males are more likely to batter their wives or girlfriends than are white males) did not originate in African tradition (Dennis, Key, Kirk, & Smith, 1995). These authors suggest that the tradition of abuse is part of the American experience. Thus we must examine the American experience of African American males when trying to interpret and intervene in the problem of spouse abuse in African American families.

Numerous attempts to explain the prevalence of domestic and other forms of violence in the black community have been offered, primarily by sociologists and criminologists. The belief that a high rate of violence among blacks is inevitable and "normal" is partly grounded in a racial stereotype. It is also a product of observations made by Eurocentric social scientists who have sought to explain disproportionate levels of violence within the black community. Historically, black women and children have been afforded less protection from abuse in the family than those in any other groups in American society. White women and children have also been underprotected, but much less so than blacks. Unless we confront and challenge persisting ideological and environmental constraints, increasing official intervention in domestic violence will merely result in an unequal race-of-victim pattern of intervention similar to that found in the handling of nonfamily criminal violence. That is, black and poor victims of family violence may be ignored, and most prevention efforts will be targeted at the white middle class.

Research also shows that other forms of violence occur all too frequently in the African American community. Community violence and homicide are both frightening forms of violence confronted by many African Americans. African American women and men and their children in inner-city areas are at greater jeopardy than their counterparts in other environments for witnessing the homicide of their adolescent sons, their spouses, or other family members and friends. African American women may also be at greater risk for battering and homicide by a spouse or male partner than are women in other settings. A dominant factor associated with homicide is poverty. Poverty appears to be more strongly associated with killings of family members and friends than killings of acquaintances. Spousal homicides tend to be associated with a belief in male dominance. Other factors associated with homicide of all types, except child homicide, are the consumption of alcohol, abuse of illicit drugs, and the presence of a gun in the home (Rosenberg, Stark, & Zahn, 1986).

The problem of interpersonal violence is clearly not unique to African American communities, but homicide is considered a major health problem in numerous black communities with a high rate of black-on-black murders. This problem is addressed only rarely in the research literature. The lack of data has led to the common misconception that violence in the black community is connected only with crime, and thus it is considered a legal rather than a health or community problem.

Several recent studies suggest that black women victims of domestic violence are more likely than white women victims to report abuse to police and to call police to resolve conflict within their intimate relationships (Hutchison, Hirschel, & Pesackis, 1994; Miller, 1989). They are also more likely to report all types of violent crime to police, compared with white women (Bachman, 1994; Bachman & Coker, 1995). This finding may be related to economic resources and social class. Women with higher incomes likely have greater access to resources to assist them in keeping their abuse private because they can afford private medical care and safe shelter. The result, according to Miller (1989), is that they are able to escape detection by law enforcement, hospital emergency rooms, or social service agencies. Thus the significance of race in the analysis of domestic violence rates may have more to do with access to resources than with race (Hampton & Gelles, 1993; Miller, 1989).

Coker (1992) reported that police were more likely to make an arrest when victims had sustained injuries, when the offender did not have a history of violence, and when black offenders were victimizing black victims (compared with white men who had victimized white women). Women who experienced repeated victimizations by the same assailant were more likely to sustain injuries than women who reported no prior history of violence by their attacker (Coker, 1992). Bachman and Coker (1995) suggested that unreported incidents not only eliminate the opportunity for offenders to receive formal sanctions but also place women at an increased risk of sustaining injury. However, because the efficacy of police and/or the judicial system in protecting women is still unproved, more research is needed to delineate systematically and carefully the effectiveness of alternative police responses in deterring incidents of domestic violence.

Sampson (1987) conducted conceptual work on exploring the relationship between African American male joblessness and urban violence of all forms. Unemployment is a risk factor for domestic violence that has been found consistently across studies (Hotaling & Sugarman, 1986; Tolman & Bennett, 1990). The extent to which negative attitudes held by whites become self-fulfilling in relation to minority groups (e.g., having more of a predilection toward violence) is also an important area for future investigation. Peterson-Lewis, Turner, and Adams (1986) suggested that African American women may attribute the causes of their abuse to the larger society but not to the abuser. They may rationalize that the abuse they have endured from mates reflects the treatment the partner received from the dominant culture. If true, this dynamic may reinforce the myth of the "strong black woman," willing and able to tolerate abuse and other indignities to protect her family and her mate. These authors concluded that African American females may believe that African American males are more likely than white males to be arrested if police intervene in domestic violence incidents and to be the victims of police maltreatment. Therefore, the women may feel terrible conflict when making decisions about calling the police.

One exceptional preventive/intervention model for dealing with black women's health problems is the National Black Women's Health Project (NBWHP). This program was initiated by the activist and advocate Billye Y. Avery, an African American grassroots organizer who has worked tirelessly since the early 1980s to help black women improve their mental and physical well-being through empowerment, healing, and self-love. The NBWHP uses a highly acclaimed model of community-based self-help programs, community-based health centers, retreats, educational films, and publications. The organization deals directly with black women's health concerns within the context of black culture. The number one health issue the project addresses is violence against black women of all ages. The NBWHP program can be duplicated anywhere. It is represented by 96 self-help groups in 22 states and 6 groups in Kenya, Barbados, and Belize (White, 1994). The work of this group has been supported by the W. K. Kellogg Foundation; Avery received the prestigious MacArthur Foundation Award.

Survey Findings Specific to African Americans

One of the overall EDK survey findings specific to African Americans is important to note as it relates to community action and education. Comparing attitudes about domestic violence by gender in the three ethnic categories, the survey found that only African American women and men appeared almost equally worried about family violence. This finding appears unrelated to education or income; thus it may be an important shared cultural perspective to consider when planning ethnic-specific interventions. African American women and men may already view this problem through the same lens (in contrast to the denial of domestic violence among many white males). One must first recognize and accept the reality that domestic violence is a serious problem before addressing solutions. Thus African American women and men may both be ready to consider specific interventions that might be relevant within their communities.

Domestic Violence in the Latino Community

The culture and current realities of Latino families also have complex interactions with domestic violence. *Marianismo* is a concept describing the expectation that Latinas will emulate the qualities of the Virgin Mary, such as moral integrity and spiritual strength. The spiritual strength should engender self-sacrifice, including tolerating her husband's bad habits, submitting to males of the family, complying with her husband's decisions, and supporting her husband unwaveringly. Family tradition and family unity are important values in the Latino community, and family loyalty is essential. Typically, Latinos value the family's well-being over an individual's *(familialism)*. Divorce is less acceptable than among Anglo populations. Traditional Latino families are hierarchical, with the elderly, parents, and males holding power and authority. Male and female roles are separated at an early age and often strictly delineated. The male is the head of the family and is expected to be strong and dominant. He assumes the role of protector of the family—particularly of females. The female is expected to be the family nurturer and submit to males. She is expected to sacrifice for the family. Family matters are handled with privacy, and serious matters such as domestic violence are often handled from within rather than from outside the family. The family, including extended family members, is seen as a source of support at all times.

The concept of *machismo* is also still present in some Latino families and communities. Machismo refers not only to the dominant role of the male but to the sense of responsibility and perhaps pride in the male role. It also represents the investment of strength in males and the need to avoid any signs of weakness.

The focus group conversations in this study revealed aspects of the machismo concept. Some Latinas strongly supported the cultural argument that men who assault their wives are actually living up to cultural perceptions encouraged by our society. They described violence as part of the macho culture. The Latinas felt that deep-rooted traditions of male dominance still exist. Latinas noted a difference between men from Mexico and those born in the United States: They felt the former were more rigid, punitive, and domineering toward women, and many attributed men's violent behavior to lack of education. Latinos were least likely to agree that the use of force was a means of compensating for the lack of other forms of power or sources of self-esteem. This again may be a result of machismo and Latino men's reluctance to admit that they use force to control women, because they view themselves as protective of women.

Many Latinos believe the universe is controlled by external forces and so is an individual's destiny. The attitude of *que sera, sera* or "what will be, will be" is widespread. Even the structure of the Spanish language protects the speaker from accepting full responsibility for unpleasantness. For example, the construction of a sentence that suggests "I missed my plane" becomes "The plane left me." The phrase avoids direct personal responsibility. The feeling that events are meant to be and cannot be changed is often strongly related to religious belief. External events are thought to be "God's will" or externally controlled. Religion has a major influence on behavior and is a source of comfort, particularly in times of stress. Religious beliefs, customs, and superstitions form an intrinsic part of family culture. Material suffering is compensated for by spiritual reward. Suffering on earth is often seen as a way to attain Heaven. Forgiveness of the offender may be perceived as mandated by God or the church.

Catholicism is historically and presently the predominant religious affiliation for Latinas. This religion considers maintaining the family unit as primary, even at the expense of a woman's well-being (Molina, Zambrana, Aguirre-Molina, 1994), which affects how Latinas may react to abuse. In one study, a higher percentage of Latinas sought assistance from religious organizations before going to a shelter (Torres, 1991). In addition, some Latinas practice *curanderismo,* which is the art and science of using herbs, prayers, and rituals to cure physical, spiritual, and emotional ills. Some who sought help from agencies had practiced curanderismo first.

Torres (1991), in one of the few ethnic group comparative studies to date, found cross-cultural differences between Latinas and Anglo-American women in terms of their attitudes toward wife abuse and their perceptions of what constitutes wife abuse; Latinas were more tolerant of wife abuse than were Anglo women. Some acts, including hitting or verbal abuse, had to occur more frequently to be considered abusive by Latinas. Furthermore, Latinas had a slightly different perception of what constitutes wife abuse. Some acts perceived as abusive by the Anglo women were not considered abusive by Latinas: for example, verbal abuse or failure to provide adequate food and shelter. The nature of abuse experienced by both groups of women was basically the same for acts considered to be physical abuse. For acts considered to be emotional abuse, Latinas showed more tolerance than Anglo-American women. However, in spite of these findings, there was no significant difference between the two groups in the severity and frequency of abuse.

The choices Latinas have in response to being abused are similar to what most Anglo women have. If a Latina leaves her home, she encounters the same problems basic to all women. Torres's (1991) study showed that culture, family, and religion were the major factors affecting how Latinas reacted to being battered.

The same study found that Latinas pointed to the family as the most important factor influencing their decision to leave or stay in a battering relationship (Torres, 1991). Latinas were more likely than Anglo women to report that they stayed in a relationship because of their children and threats to family members, whereas Anglo women reported staying because of love or not having a place to go. Some 40% of Latinas, compared with 20% of Anglo women, said they left because of their children. The reason most frequently given by Latinas for going back to their spouses was "the children." Compared with Anglo women, Latinas in the Torres study tended to stay longer in the relationship with their abusive spouses before seeking assistance, because of family pressure and "for the sake of the children." The study also found that Latinas were hit more frequently in front of family members than were Anglo women. Latinas left and came back to their spouses more times than Anglo women. Thus it is important not to assume that because a battered Latina has asked for help that she will want to leave her home.

Therefore, advocates and professionals working with battered Latinas should be aware of the family roles, traditions, and expectations idiosyncratic to the Latino culture. The attitudes a woman's culture holds about sex roles affect a woman's self-image. In addition, the study reported that Latinas were especially sensitive and reacted to criticism or nonacceptance (perceived or imagined) of themselves, or their family, culture, language, husband (or other male relative), economic situation, level of education, consciousness, and/or degree of dependence/independence.

Survey Findings Specific to Latino Culture

As noted in the Introduction, there has been minimal involvement by Latino men and women in the battered women's movement. However, the EDK survey found more overall similarities than differences among ethnic/racial groups regarding perceptions of the extent of domestic violence in their own personal experience. Two areas of findings regarding concern about the growth of family violence in the Latino community deserve specific comment.

First, in the EDK study, Latinas were the group most worried about the growth of family violence. One could speculate several causes, such as exposure to violence, the media, or education. Latinas in the United States have a lower educational level than Caucasian women, and education level was found to be related to concern about domestic violence in this study.

Second, Latinas were more concerned about the growth of domestic violence than were Latino men (43% vs. 35%), a difference similar to but smaller than that between Caucasian women and men in the EDK poll. Although both men (64%) and women (70%) acknowledged that men beat women, Latinas were more likely than their male counterparts to say that it happens often (42% vs. 28%). However, Latinos were least likely to deny that men rarely beat women (26% compared with 62% of Caucasians, 53% of African Americans, and 43% of Asian Americans). Thus it is possible that even though Latinos were willing to admit that violence occurs in the home, these men might minimize it, whereas women were more apt to admit the frequency of the abuse. Perhaps the minimizing is part of the macho image and the protective role that Latinos assume over Latinas. In addition, Latinas were more likely than their male counterparts to agree that men beating women is a behavior learned in the home (41% vs. 27%).

Although the majority of every group agreed that a man threatening a woman constituted a public matter, there were significant racial/ethnic differences. Caucasians were most likely to say it is a public matter (67%), whereas Latinos (51%) were least likely. Again, this is indicative of the Latino culture, where family matters are handled in privacy.

Across race, class, and ethnic groups, there was strong agreement with the statement that beating up a woman is often learned in the home. There were significant gender differences among Caucasians (57% of women vs. 44% of men strongly agreed) and among Latinos (41% vs. 27%).

In the focus groups, most men and women agreed with the statement that domestic violence is an attack on women's dignity and freedom; women tended to agree strongly more often than men. In the EDK survey, there were also significant gender differences among Caucasians (59% of women vs. 39% of men strongly agreed) and Latinos (43% vs. 24% strongly agree). There were also differences across racial/ethnic groups. White women were most likely to agree strongly with this statement (59% compared with 43% of Latinas, 38% of African Americans, and 25% of Asian American women). Among men, Latinos were significantly less likely to agree strongly with this statement than were men from other racial and ethnic groups. Latinas agreed with the statement, but blamed the victim for letting the man rob her of her self-esteem. Similarly, several Latinos said the loss of a woman's confidence depended on her spirit.

In summary, these findings suggest that Latinas are more open than Latinos to revealing the issues and circumstances related to domestic violence. As a group, this population is also less likely than others to be concerned about domestic violence or to think it should be a public issue.

Domestic Violence in the Asian American Community

Asia is home to some of the oldest continuous civilizations in the world. In China, India, and other Asian countries, patriarchal relationships define women's roles in society and are reinforced through language, laws, religion, daily customs, and beliefs. Both the Asian community and outsiders view Asian culture as it was defined by men centuries ago, without regard to the views of women from those cultures nor to the reality that culture undergoes constant change and evolution.

In developing strategies to change perceptions about domestic violence among Asian Americans, understanding the deep roots of Asian belief systems is key to creating a strategy that both incorporates culture and challenges traditional values that condone domestic violence.

In an attempt to be culturally sensitive, some experts mistakenly incorporate a stereotypical, static view of Asian culture and beliefs to inform their analysis or strategy for addressing domestic violence. One example of this can be seen in the Dong Lau Chen case, in which a Chinese immigrant man in New York beat his wife to death with a hammer in 1987. Dong Lau Chen defended his actions by stating that in China, if a man believes his wife to be unfaithful, he has the right to kill her because she has brought shame upon him. Professor Pasternak from Hunter College provided expert testimony to verify that Chen's statement and actions under the circumstances were that of a "reasonable Chinese man." The judge in this case sentenced Chen to 5 years of probation, with no jail time or fines (Volpp, 1994).

Many Asian Americans protested the sentence. No experts were called by the prosecution, and if more research had been done on current Chinese laws against domestic violence, it would have come to light that the beliefs Chen described reflected *feudal* China. In present-day China, strict laws exist that make domestic violence, from battery to murder, a crime.

The author and other Asian American domestic violence workers from the Asian Women's Shelter in San Francisco and the New York Asian Women's Center attended the NGO Forum and United Nations Fourth World Conference on Women in Beijing, in August 1995. At a bilingual workshop, the Asian American women shared the story of the Dong Lau Chen case with the Chinese women there, and the Chinese women were shocked. They reported that the same type of domestic violence murder in China would likely draw a severe sentence, and that laws against domestic violence have been in effect in their country since 1949.

The first shelters for battered women appeared in the United States during the 1970s; the earliest shelter probably existed in 13th-century Japan. Kakeko-midera (refuge temple) in the city of Kamakura, Kanagawa Prefecture, was a safe refuge where women could flee their husbands. Divorce in medieval times was virtually unheard of, but if a woman served in the temple for 3 years, she could be officially granted a divorce (Kanagawa Women's Council, 1995).

One of the few small-scale societies with *no* wife beating, according to anthropological evidence reported in Levinson's (1989) study of family violence across cultures, exists in central Thailand. Levinson attributed the lack of family violence to the group's practice of nonviolence throughout their society and to the equal distribution of labor and power without differentiation along gender lines.

As stated in Chapter 1, sanctions against battering are seen to be important deterrents to the escalation of domestic violence. Many examples can be drawn from traditional Asian communities throughout history, continuing to the present day. A modern example of public sanctions is Jagori, a single women's group in a village near New Delhi, India; members of the group have held protests in front of the homes of batterers to shame them publicly and raise community awareness and support. Another example is in Beijing, where batterers are held accountable through sanctions from their neighborhood block captains, work unit, and/or the criminal justice system.

Historical examples of public opposition to domestic violence among Asians are important in demonstrating not only that domestic violence is a global problem, but that efforts to prevent domestic violence are global as well. The seeds of changing public perception about domestic violence are rooted in every cultural history.

Survey Findings Specific to Asian Americans

In terms of saliency of domestic violence, Table 1.4 showed that Asian Americans were the least likely of the ethnic groups to be "very worried" (20% of women and 26% of men) about the growth of family violence and the most likely of any ethnic group to be "not worried" (30% of women and 28% of men).

This low rate of concern for the growth of family violence among Asian Americans could be attributed to the lack of public awareness about the issue. Asian Americans have traditionally kept problems within the family. Extended families are common in Asian cultures and are an excellent network of support when they operate in healthy ways. When family violence exists, however, the extended family can be a further barrier for a battered woman to seek outside help and for outside community members to become aware that the problem of family violence exists.

Contributing to the invisibility of family violence within the Asian American community is the severe lack of resources for Asian American battered women who want to escape violent relationships. Racism, the lack of bilingual/bicultural programs, and anti-immigrant sentiment all contribute to silencing Asian American battered women.

Once appropriate resources are made available, Asian American battered women respond as much as battered women from other ethnic groups. The Asian Women's Shelter in San Francisco turns away about 75% of the battered women who call in need of shelter because of lack of space. Some 80% of the shelter's residents choose to end their relationship with the batterer and rebuild their lives as single women and mothers. The few other shelters (New York Asian Women's Center; Center for the Pacific Asian Family, Los Angeles) in the United States that provide bilingual/bicultural services to Asian American battered women and their children report similar numbers of Asian American women requesting services and choosing to end relationships with the batterer.

Although the difference was not statistically significant, Asian American women in the EDK survey were the only group of women "not worried" about the growth of family violence at a higher percentage than men of the same ethnicity (30% compared with 28%), and Asian American women were the only group of women to have fewer "very worried" responses than the men in their same ethnic group (20% compared with 26%).

Asian Americans in the EDK survey also differed from their ethnic counterparts along gender lines in their responses to the statement that domestic violence is an attack on women's dignity and freedom. While in other ethnic groups, women tended to agree with this statement more often than men, for Asian Americans, the men were more likely than the women to agree strongly with this statement (39% compared with 25%). A possible insight into the women's relatively low degree of agreement with this statement was revealed in focus group conversations in which Asian American women did not think most Asians focused on words like *self-esteem* and *self-confidence*. Perhaps they felt that words such as *freedom, independence,* and *self* place too much emphasis on individualism. Asian cultures and languages often express values of interdependence and interconnection. This does not necessarily mean that Asian American women do not believe in concepts such as self-esteem and freedom, but words such as women's *confidence, strength,* and *rights* might resonate more clearly among Asian American women.

The EDK study was among the first to include Asian Americans in a breakdown of responses by ethnicity. Further research is important to gain more comparison data about Asian Americans' perceptions about family violence and to provide more insight into the responses by Asian Americans in this study, particularly when they differed from the responses from all other ethnic groups.

Community Response to Battered Women of Color

Some ethnic minority communities encourage the victim to keep silent and to deny her abuse. However, this also happens in some white families; comparative proportions are unknown. One often hears of the family of color in which people are abused, and one way they deal with it is to encourage the victim to remain silent. In Latino communities, if a wife is abused, she will often say "My mother told me, 'You married him. You made your bed; you lie in it,' and I will have to stay in it."

The resulting embarrassment and perceived stigma might keep the family from doing anything. This is especially true if the family tried to get assistance in the past and was unsuccessful, or if the family was met with discrimination. In some cases, women who are abused by their husbands won't tell their family or won't tell anybody else for fear their family or their brother or someone close would get into a fight with the husband. Therefore, they will often pretend there is nothing going on. This can also happen when a person is abused by someone outside of the family or by a coworker.

Thus discrimination against the subgroup occurs as an outcome modifier. Studies have found that special populations of women tend to be abused over and over. These victims are often minority women, the homeless, the mentally ill, or other multiply stigmatized women.

Some victims experience secondary injuries. When they are abused and go to the health care system or call the police for assistance, they often experience discrimination. Women of color can often be especially sensitive and reactive to criticism or perceived nonacceptance of themselves, their family, culture, and language because of prior experience with racist or insensitive mainstream institutions.

Interventions for Women of Color

Intervention policies and practices for treating wife abuse should accommodate the diverse cultural backgrounds of battered women. Our society has a responsibility and an obligation to deliver services to all battered women without regard to racial or ethnic background. At the same time, we need to recognize the important differences among cultural groups and be careful about assumptions.

Some of the culturally specific interventions initiatives needed are to:

- Improve the management and treatment of victims of violence
- Increase the ability of the health care system to recognize and treat consequences of violence and other injuries
- Improve the identification and treatment of perpetrators of violence by the health care system
- Decrease financial barriers to care for victims

Women of color often can't afford to go to a counselor or pay for their expenses.

More research is needed on the emotional effects of violence among minorities. One of the few areas of research on culturally specific mental health effects was conducted with Vietnam veterans, among whom blacks and Latinos had a higher rate of post-traumatic stress disorder (Marsella, Friedman, Gerrity, & Scurfield, 1996). The researchers concluded that, because the minorities were brought up under stressful conditions, when they were exposed to traumatic stress they reacted differently. If true for minority Vietnam veterans, it may also be true for victimized women of color.

In working with battered women of color, it is necessary to be aware of the family roles, traditions, and expectations that are unique to their culture. Some of these women may be victims of racial prejudice by majority group members, which make family and community ties all the more important. What kind of service they will receive and how effective advocates and professionals will be in their treatment of battered women of color will depend on the degree of knowledge about each group's cultural values, genuine concern and caring for patients of that ethnicity, and willingness to respect and use cultural values whenever these values are not detrimental to the individual.

Those who do not speak English are particularly at risk for poor service. English-speaking professionals and advocates need to be aware of possible language differences. Even if a woman of color is bilingual, it may be difficult for her to express feelings or details of abuse when she is under stress. She may not understand professional jargon. Interventions, when possible, should be conducted in the individual's native language.

Presenting an alternative to existing explanations and institutional responses to wife abuse means that we must adopt alternative methods, explanations, and solutions to the problem. The methods must be concrete and include awareness of historical and contemporary contexts. The explanations must consider why wife beating has occurred and continues as a recurrent pattern within the traditional fabric of society and how it operates and is supported by institutional ideologies and responses. The proposed solutions must include short- and long-term alternatives that challenge existing ideologies and institutional responses. This overall alternative enterprise must operate on at least three interrelated levels: individual, ideological, and institutional.

Changing Public Perceptions of Domestic Violence in Communities of Color: The Message and the Messenger

Respondents to the EDK survey and focus group participants demonstrated a reluctance to attribute causation for domestic violence, and no clear-cut causative factors emerged. Given the complex intersection of race, gender, and culture on perceptions of domestic violence, and the difficulty of developing values and norms that reflect the multicultural reality of being a person of color in the United States, it is not surprising that responses from both male and female minority group participants were mixed.

These survey and focus group results suggest that public messages should not stress any particular causative factor but should emphasize the sentiment that "no matter what the reason, domestic violence is wrong and cannot be tolerated." This message would be effective in any ethnic minority community but only if delivered in a manner that clearly indicated that members of the particular group were not exceptions to the message.

Growing up without images, words, stories, movies, songs, and other popular messages that reflect the reality of that person's, family's, or community's ethnic background, Asian Americans and other marginalized groups in the United States are used to interpreting public messages as exclusive. Only in recent years have the media become more culturally diversified, but African Americans are generally the only ethnic group regularly represented, and they are often portrayed stereotypically. Regarding an issue that people do not want to face, such as domestic violence, the message must clearly indicate that it is relevant to each minority community.

A model for ethnically diverse public education can be found in the anti-smoking campaign launched in California. The public message cautioned people about the effects of first- and second-hand smoke. The message was tailored to various Asian groups, with billboards and bus shelters featuring images of Asian children and captions in several Asian languages, including Korean, Vietnamese, and Chinese. These messages effectively addressed Asian values about the "family before the individual" and clearly connected the problem with the targeted community audience. Thus effective messages need to be culturally sensitive and appropriate to the needs of each community. Just translating messages that have been developed for the mainstream community will not meet the needs of another language community.

There is a growing awareness within African American communities that violence is a matter of great concern, particularly because the violence in these communities is often perpetrated by young people who are also its most likely victims. Recognizing that domestic violence, primarily violence against women and children, occurs in every racial and economic echelon of society should not minimize the fact that domestic violence occurs much too frequently among African Americans. Domestic violence needs to be considered in terms of both its commonalities with the more general violence problem and its differences. Additional research could help define policy and structure interventions to best address issues of domestic violence and violence of all forms in the African American community.

Formulating clear answers about the nature and contributing causes of domestic violence in the African American community will take time. Meanwhile, it is imperative that African Americans confront the current reality and severity of domestic violence. Data currently available suggest a need to focus on male violence directed against women, children, youth, and adult males (Tomes, 1995). Regardless of cause (external or internal, situational or institutional), African Americans must perceive domestic violence and all forms of violence within their communities as intolerable. They must respond to the problem proactively. Recent public awareness initiatives, changes in public policy at the national level, and changes in state legislation and in the criminal justice and social services agencies have all helped to focus the attention of African Americans on the serious problems of domestic and other forms of violence.

Community Education and Prevention Efforts

Efforts aimed at the prevention of family violence, in particular victim assistance programs for women, have not effectively helped minorities. Educational programs are needed that teach conflict resolution, stress management, and coping skills; that offer self-help groups and educational programs about family life, family planning, and child rearing; and that support families with community-based organizations.

Despite the many barriers and the complex factors to consider when developing community education and prevention efforts in each of the minority ethnic communities, advocates *have* developed some innovative and effective strategies. Successful community-based programs tend to be designed using intimate knowledge of and respect for the cultural heritage of the participants. Domestic violence prevention programs could follow models used successfully to deal with similar problems. We must continue efforts aimed at developing community institutions and support systems, public consciousness raising, and education.

There is growing evidence that African Americans are interested in and willing to develop community institutions and support systems (e.g., Neighborhood Crime Watch Programs) to prevent black-on-black violence (Bell, 1987). As the current research suggests, few respondents, African Americans not excepted, were unwilling to excuse a batterer's behavior. Strong community sanctions against perpetrators of domestic violence are needed. Established black institutions such as churches, colleges, civil rights organizations, and beauty parlors/barbershops may need the support of the larger community to address the issue of violence adequately.

Few programs focus directly on prevention of and intervention in violence in the Latino community. Some programs have been developed to deal with violence in general. Few shelters exist in the United States exclusively for Latinas in battering relationships (two in Arizona and one in California). These shelters have attempted to deliver services that are culturally specific. Other programs in shelters provide bilingual services and translations of the Anglo model to work with battered women instead of developing culturally appropriate services.

The same is true for programs that focus on men who have battered. Most of the programs in the United States are adapted from Anglo programs rather than developed specifically to meet the needs of Latino, African American, or Asian American men (Williams & Becker, 1994).

Many Asian Americans remain uneducated about domestic violence. Racism, anti-immigrant sentiment, and cultural freeze add to the complexity of addressing the issue. The Asian American population, however, is not monolithic, and many Asian Americans are actively changing public perceptions and resources regarding domestic violence. One example is the San Francisco Filipina Advisory Committee (FAC). The committee, originally made up of former residents of the Asian Women's Shelter, staff, board, and community members, collaborated on a handbook, *A Community Secret,* by FAC member Jacqueline Agtuca. The book was distributed throughout the Filipino community and was designed to tell in novella fashion the story of two Filipina domestic violence survivors, interspersed with facts and resources. It was an immediate success, and a second, revised edition was published by Seal Press (Agtuca, 1994). The FAC has continued to grow, and in 1995, with support from the Family Violence Prevention Fund, it held "Pagbubuklod at Pagbabago: Coming Together for Change," the first conference dedicated to addressing domestic violence in the Filipino community. Leaders from the Filipino community were invited to participate and are part of a growing number of people dedicated to increasing awareness of and effective responses to domestic violence in their community.

In Boston, Cambodian community leaders, formerly battered women, social work students, and others joined forces to create a video about domestic violence in the Cambodian community. The video incorporates Cambodian religious, family, and community values to send the message that domestic violence destroys us all. A copy was recently brought to Cambodia to assist women who are developing that country's first domestic violence services.

In Oakland, California, a small but powerful movement is building to address domestic violence in the Iu Mien community. When Mayseng Saetern began her work as women's advocate at the Asian Women's Shelter in 1989, she was probably the first Mien person to work in the field of domestic violence. As a child in Laos, Mayseng reports that she was disturbed and frightened by the prevalence of domestic violence in her village and felt helpless in changing the situation. Her response parallels the feelings of children living in violent homes, and although Mayseng did not experience family violence directly, she felt the consequences as a member of a close-knit community. As a domestic violence advocate, she has built upon the strengths of her Mien community in Oakland to raise accountability regarding domestic violence. Mayseng balances the risks of challenging traditional values, as well as her personal safety, with the commitment to changing beliefs and responding to domestic violence in her community.

Summary

Successful models of domestic violence education for all three communities of color explored in this chapter emphasize our common traditional values of family and community and challenge values that perpetuate and condone domestic violence. These strategies avoid putting forward one issue at the expense of another (e.g., women's issues over race issues) and instead address their intersection. The resulting projects effectively raise awareness and break through denial of domestic violence. By emerging from the community they target, the strategies have the most potential to reach the community and create lasting change. These models, and others from diverse communities, must be understood as central to a larger national and international shift in public beliefs and actions regarding domestic violence. To view minority communities as "special populations" further marginalizes the identified groups and weakens the power of a broad public message. Financial support for prevention and education efforts is extremely limited, yet it is a critical investment for our future.

It is critical to extend help (resources) to ethnic minority groups in a way that respects their history, values, and needs as they struggle to deal with violence. Incorporating ethnic-specific approaches centrally into a national strategy and directly addressing racism and anti-immigrant sentiments as they intersect with domestic violence can create the diversity necessary to resonate with the diversity of this nation's people and bring home the same message: There is no excuse for domestic violence. Like water on rock, a constant, flowing movement can build momentum and old values can be worn away. Drop by drop, community by community, perceptions and values can change.

Public Education Campaigns on Domestic Violence

Crafting Effective Messages
to Promote a Cultural Change

Every week, the media bear tidings of yet another domestic homicide in which an estranged husband has killed his spouse or girlfriend, often in front of their children. After 20 years of grassroots organizing, the growth of a coalition against domestic violence in every state, and the establishment of more than 1,800 domestic violence programs across the country, we must ask ourselves how such horrifying acts can continue to take place. The remedies that have grown out of the domestic violence movement, which focus primarily on victim services and criminal justice response, are critical in ensuring the safety of women and children, but, unfortunately, they are not enough: Almost 4 million women are abused in a single year (Harris, 1993), and 42% of murdered women are killed by the men who promised to love them (University of Colorado, 1994).

One reason that domestic violence continues to flourish is because of the subtle but pervasive ways that American society implicitly accepts and condones disrespect of and violence against women. Over the years, the implicit cultural acceptance of violence against women has been reflected in the way the justice system has historically—and until recently—responded to domestic violence. Typically, police called to deal with an incident of abuse did not take the problem seriously, rarely arresting perpetrators. When battered women persevered and tried to press charges, district attorneys often refused to support their cases, and those cases that made it to court were likely to be dismissed. In domestic violence incidents, the general attitude was "she provoked it," "it's a private, family problem, not our business," "there's nothing really wrong with a husband showing he's boss," or "if it was really so bad, why didn't she just leave?"

The cultural climate about women has improved in some ways in the past two decades. Women have made gains in the workforce, for example, and the justice system takes domestic violence more seriously. In some states, clearer procedures and stronger laws now exist so that police officers and judges can react swiftly and appropriately. More shelters are available. And public attitudes *have* changed dramatically. As discussed in Chapter 4, our research indicates that as of November 1995, 82% of Americans believe outside intervention is necessary if a husband hits his wife—even if she is not physically injured—and virtually everyone (96%) believes outside intervention is necessary if he inflicts injuries that require medical attention. People are beginning to recognize their *own* role in stopping domestic violence, asking "What can *I* do to help?" rather than "What should *she* do to escape the abuse?"

However, the vast majority of Americans hold covert attitudes that condone battering and help create an environment in which inaction is the norm rather than the exception. As reported earlier, the November 1995 Lieberman poll also found that almost half of the American public (46%) currently believes that men sometimes physically abuse women because they are stressed out or drunk, not because they intend to hurt them. This widely held excuse for battering helps explain how friends, family, and institutions can continue to resist holding men accountable for their behavior.

The following anecdote is instructive.

> Ed is a liberal individual who is very progressive on social issues. He mentioned to a woman friend (a domestic violence activist) that he had just made a startling discovery—a man with whom he plays weekly basketball regularly beats up his wife. Ed's woman friend asked him why he continues to play basketball with that kind of person. "Because," Ed replied, "he's basically a nice guy."

Highly publicized cases from around the country indicate that as far as the courts are concerned, judges still have much to learn about domestic violence. In the state of Maryland, for example, a judge recently imposed a sentence of only 18 months on a man who shot his wife in the head with a rifle after finding her with another man. The judge stated, "I seriously wonder how many men . . . would have the strength to walk away without inflicting some corporal punishment. I'm forced to impose a sentence—only because I think I must do it to make the system honest."

Even though the staggering numbers of abused women indicate that progress is slow, we know that what is learned can be unlearned. Broad cultural messages about male-female relationships can be changed; attitudes about what is acceptable behavior can be reframed; children growing up with domestic violence can be taught new behaviors. Domestic violence can be positioned not only as an issue that touches the lives of more than just abused women and batterers but also as a problem that tears families and communities apart and fills our courtrooms, hospitals, and morgues. In order to galvanize Americans to take action on this important problem, we must identify domestic violence as an issue that individuals and communities alike can—and must—address. We must educate people to recognize that they have a role in helping battered women and their children, teach them that their behavior matters, and show them how to get involved. The strategic use of communications can play a key role in raising public awareness, changing attitudes, and promoting personal and community involvement. To be effective, communications strategies must be aimed at countering the existing cultural acceptance of violence and, instead, producing public outrage about and a commitment to stop violence against women.

People can learn. They can change the way they think *and* behave. Witness the success of prevention programs aimed at raising awareness about recycling, cigarette smoking, and drunk driving.

Social Change Movements

Other social change movements have successfully affected public behavior involving important issues, and we can learn from them and apply their lessons to the issue of domestic violence. We can apply the knowledge gained through the successes of these other social movements. Recycling is now a part of the everyday lives and habits of most Americans as a result of high-exposure media efforts to educate the public about the environment. Attitudes about smoking have changed from viewing it as glamorous, sophisticated behavior (validated by seeing our favorite movie stars lighting up on the big screen) to seeing it as dangerous (with activists boycotting movies in which smoking is glamorized). In California, where there have been massive public education efforts to caution the public about the first- and second-hand effects of smoking, the number of smokers declined from 26% in 1987 to 21% in 1990 (Kizer & Honig, 1990). Finally, our attitudes about drinking and driving have also been transformed by pervasive public education efforts. People have learned to watch out for potential perpetrators and to take responsibility for preventing the problem (by taking the key away from a friend too intoxicated to drive or assigning a designated, nondrinking driver).

Saturating the media with messages that promote individual involvement and action—even when the messages are unpleasant and intrusive—is an effective method for changing behavior. For example, a public service advertising campaign sponsored by the Advertising Council urged people, particularly men, to speak to their doctors about the difficult subject of colon cancer. The campaign increased awareness about the issue from 11% to 29% after only 6 months of high exposure to advertising, and up to 40% in 12 months. The total number of people who spoke to their doctors about colon cancer during the course of the education effort increased by 43%, 114% for men (Advertising Research Foundation, 1991). Because colon cancer is a disease with a good prognosis after early treatment, we can safely assume that this media campaign effort has actually saved lives.

Public education efforts that have succeeded in producing these kinds of significant changes in behavior and attitudes about difficult subjects have several common threads. First, each of them developed simple, powerful messages that are action-oriented, emotional, empowering, and short. For example, "Save the planet," "Friends don't let friends drive drunk," and so on. Second, these initiatives have relied on a clear understanding of their audience, using focus groups, polling data, and tracking surveys to measure attitudes, reported behavior, and responses to campaign messages. Third, all the campaigns addressed issues that could be seen by almost everyone through the lens of their own personal experience. For example, most people have coughed from cigarette smoke at some point or been afraid of being killed or disabled by a drunk driver. Little explanation is necessary. Through experience, people already understand the issue and are hooked emotionally.

In addition, these campaigns clearly communicated the benefits associated with behavior change, a particularly critical aspect of public education efforts when the desired outcome requires a difficult adjustment in behavior. The campaigns against AIDS and cigarette smoking, for instance, have relied on messages that communicated clearly the hazards of *not* adapting desired behavior changes (i.e., risk of contracting deadly diseases like AIDS or lung cancer).

Each of these movements also used the media to convey their public health and public policy messages. None would have succeeded without strong press support. Most of the campaigns also enjoyed visible support from powerful opinion leaders who have the ability to generate press attention, make policy changes, and assist financially. Finally, sustained leadership is essential; either institutions or charismatic leaders must guide the effort on a sustained basis to make steady progress toward its objectives.

In the area of domestic violence, if advocates want to see a lasting difference in behavior—and ensure that domestic violence is not merely this year's fad—they must make a concerted effort to address the public's subtle acceptance of, and turning away from, the problem. Legal sanctions are not enough. We must launch massive public education initiatives to encourage individuals and communities to claim *personal responsibility* for stopping domestic violence, just as they have taken responsibility for reducing drunk driving and protecting the environment. Americans must be encouraged to condemn abusive behavior at every turn and to assist battered women getting the help they need to stay safe.

Developing a Message

As with other campaigns, developing a message for such initiatives must be grounded in a clear understanding of what would motivate the target audience to get involved in stopping domestic violence. Some messages may prove effective with one subset of the target population and not another. For example, developing messages that emphasize the devastating impact of domestic violence on people's lives may work well when aimed at individuals who have a friend, daughter, or coworker who is a victim (or perpetrator) of domestic violence. But these same people might not necessarily be motivated to get involved through appeals based on the enormous impact of the problem on the legal, medical, and social service systems (although still other groups, namely policymakers, might respond to exactly these types of messages). Other populations might be persuaded to get involved because of perceived links between domestic violence and youth violence, or out of a sense of basic fairness and a conviction about the equality of women. Indeed, some individuals may be motivated to act simply by the power of the spokesperson delivering the message (as when Magic Johnson revealed his HIV-positive status). Research examining such motivating factors must look at differences between men and women, as well as race and class differences, so that messages can be tailored and targeted appropriately.

In addition to examining what some of the motivating factors are, advocates must examine some of the *barriers* to intervention for different target audiences and develop messages that address those barriers in order to promote action. Twenty years ago, it was much more difficult to mobilize the general public because of a pervasive lack of awareness about the seriousness and prevalence of domestic violence. Today that is no longer the case. But barriers remain.

The Lieberman polls clearly identify two major barriers to intervention on the issue of domestic violence. One significant reason Americans aren't currently apt to get involved is that *they don't know what to do* to make an impact. In November 1995, more than half (55%) of respondents said they didn't know what to do to reduce violence in their communities—and although this percentage is down from the 63% measured by the Lieberman poll in July 1994, lack of knowledge about what to do clearly remains a problem. Fear for one's personal safety is another reason people aren't getting involved—a striking 84% of respondents to the Lieberman poll in November 1995 said they would be concerned about their own safety if they tried to stop a specific domestic violence situation. Advocates agree not only that intervening in an ongoing instance of domestic violence can put someone in jeopardy but also that there are a whole host of ways for people to get involved that don't put them at risk. Our challenge is to let the public know what they are.

These findings have important implications for public education efforts on domestic violence. Campaigns must address these barriers to intervention if we hope to galvanize the public to action. Campaign messages must include specific information about how people can get involved (i.e., what they can do about the problem) and make it clear that these steps are effective and safe.

In addition, we must pay attention to the emotional and psychological needs of the target audience and frame the issue accordingly. For example, although evidence indicates that an overwhelming majority of domestic violence perpetrators are male, our research demonstrated consistently that both women and men strongly resist labeling men as "the enemy," wanting instead to see them as part of the solution. Campaigns that encourage men to hold other men accountable for their violence are therefore likely to be successful; those that indiscriminately blame all men for the problem are not.

Any public education strategy must address differences among various communities, particularly communities of color. Such strategies must grow out of, and be in tune with, those communities. Previous campaigns have succeeded in effecting widespread behavior change in different communities in part because messages, interventions, and sanctions have come directly from the target community. Research on AIDS prevention conducted in low-income housing projects in Chicago, for example, found that African American women were significantly more likely to adapt desired behaviors (e.g., testing for HIV antibodies, requesting condoms) in response to culturally sensitive messages about AIDS (Kalichman, Kelly, Hunter, Murphy, & Tyler, 1993). A recent report from the Center for AIDS Prevention at the University of California, San Francisco, also demonstrated that carefully focused, targeted campaigns can help stem the tide of AIDS worldwide (Stryker et al., 1995). Positive outcomes occurred because the messages were so closely tailored to the target population and because the suggested interventions were appropriate to that group's needs and behaviors.

We must apply these lessons to public education initiatives on domestic violence and pay attention to cultural differences in attitudes about the acceptability of domestic violence. Public education efforts must assess which spokespeople would be most effective with different communities and enable each community to "own" the issue, so that they develop *their own* approaches to solving the problem. We must also provide the necessary resources to accomplish this goal.

National Public Education Campaign

On the basis of the EDK focus groups and subsequent survey, the Family Violence Prevention Fund launched a national public education campaign against domestic violence in July 1994. Called *There's No Excuse for Domestic Violence,* the fund's multiyear effort aims to reduce and prevent domestic violence by educating the American public about violence against women and motivating individuals to help stop it. Sponsored by the Advertising Council and selected as its major public education and research initiative for several years, the campaign is giving unprecedented visibility to the issue.

The first phase of the campaign focused on developing advertisements addressing the seriousness and lethal nature of domestic violence. This strategic decision was made based on the EDK survey findings, which showed that most respondents believe domestic violence crosses the line from a private to a public issue when injury occurs. As discussed in Chapter 4, respondents condemned such abusive behavior as shouting, threatening, grabbing, and shoving, but they nevertheless did not believe any public interventions were necessary until injury occurred. The campaign was therefore designed to capitalize on the public's threshold for action by focusing on extremely violent behavior and killing.

As a part of the public education initiative, the Family Violence Prevention Fund developed print, radio, and television public service announcements (PSAs), as well as bus shelter and billboard displays, targeting the general public. These ads carry the campaign's key messages that "domestic violence is everybody's business" and "there's no excuse for it." In one powerful 30-second television spot called *Neighbors,* viewers see a couple in their bed listening to the sounds of a man brutally beating a woman in the apartment above them. The couple exchange anxious looks, but when the husband reaches over to the night table, instead of picking up the phone to call the police, he turns off the light. The screen fades to black and viewers are told, "It *is* your business." The corresponding newspaper piece shows a man beating a woman, along with a header reading, "If the noise coming from next door were loud music, you'd do something about it."

The television PSA fared extremely well in a pretest, generating a recall score 15% above the average of other Ad Council campaigns. Many people remembered the slogan "It is your business" in particular and understood that it meant "We should all get involved." In addition, the PSA had a positive impact on key consumer attitudes—the commercial was found to be believable (84%), important (83%), effective (76%), and thought-provoking (64%). What's more, data collected by Lieberman Research indicates that the campaign is having an impact on attitudes and behavior: Survey respondents in media markets that received heaviest exposure to the campaign were more likely than others to (a) recall the PSAs, (b) report increased action against domestic violence, (c) perceive domestic violence as an important social issue, and (d) believe that physical abusers should be arrested and incarcerated. In these heavily-exposed markets, the percentage of respondents who said they had taken action against domestic violence increased by 12 percentage points to 26% between July 1994 and November 1995.

Since its launch, the *There's No Excuse* campaign has generated more than $40 million in donated media space for the PSAs, enabling campaign messages to appear in national news magazines, on prime-time network television, in national and local newspapers, and on radio stations across the country. Already, the media have demonstrated an enormous interest in promoting a focus on what individuals can do about domestic violence, airing the television PSAs an astounding 14,000 times during the first 4 months of the campaign (Ad Council campaigns average 1,100 PSAs aired per month).

The trial of O. J. Simpson for the murders of his ex-wife and her friend and the revelations of his previous violence toward her have also focused national attention on the issue of domestic violence. A media audit conducted for the Family Violence Prevention Fund reveals that there was a dramatic increase in both television and print coverage of domestic violence in the months following O. J. Simpson's arrest and the subsequent revelations of his abuse of his ex-wife. During April and May 1994, a total of two stories about domestic violence appeared on the three networks' evening news, and a *Lexis-Nexis* search found 206 print stories that referred to domestic violence, spousal abuse, and/or battered women (PR Solutions, 1995). During June and July 1994, however, the number of network news stories skyrocketed to 54 and the *Lexis-Nexis* search uncovered 454 print stories about domestic violence. This dramatic increase in coverage was sustained through the end of 1994.

Because Simpson was such a beloved public figure, during this time period journalists began increasingly to explore the question of how violent incidents might be circumvented earlier in the cycle of abuse. The February 20, 1995, issue of *People,* for example, featured a cover story called "Why Nobody Helped Nicole: Friends, family, and police saw her bruises but failed to stop O. J.'s abuse. What went wrong?" The November 1994 issue of *Self* included an article entitled "60 Ways to Stop Domestic Violence." *Emerge* ran a piece in its September 1994 issue called "The Brutal Truth: Putting Domestic Violence on the Black Agenda," and the October 1994 issue of *Men's Fitness* ran a special report called "Is Someone You Know a Batterer? Domestic abuse is every man's problem. Here's how to spot it and stop it." In short, the events of 1994-1995 prompted a public shift toward questioning how to stop domestic violence.

Battered women across the country benefited from this exposure. Evidence suggests that battered women are more likely to seek outside intervention or leave their abusers when they perceive themselves as having resources and options for ending the violence. During the same period when domestic abuse was featured prominently in national and local media markets, including scores of articles about what to do if you are a victim, battered women across the country began seeking outside intervention in record numbers. In San Francisco alone, there was a 51% increase in the number of people calling crisis lines in the first 3 months after Nicole Brown Simpson's murder and the accompanying publicity. In the same period, 39% more people sought help from local domestic violence agencies (San Francisco Domestic Violence Consortium, 1995).

As discussed earlier, the pervasive media coverage also had a dramatic effect on the general public's perception of the problem of domestic violence. In January 1995, *Time*/CNN released findings from a poll of 1,000 adults between January 11 and 12. In comparison to the 1992 EDK poll, which found that 87% of the public considered domestic violence a serious problem, this study found that 96% of Americans considered domestic violence a serious problem in today's society. The same poll revealed that 67% of men and 80% of women viewed domestic violence as a *very* serious problem.

In addition, several studies have emerged that continue to indicate that overwhelming numbers of Americans have faced this problem. A poll conducted in 1994 for Liz Claiborne, Inc., reported that two in five (40%) corporate leaders were personally aware of employees in their company who had been affected by domestic violence. And the Time/CNN poll of January 11 to 12, 1995, found that 57% of respondents said they personally knew a victim of domestic violence.

But despite these impressive numbers and despite public recognition of domestic violence as a serious problem, until recently, few people had actually taken any action against domestic violence. Lieberman Research data collected in July 1994 revealed that 29% of respondents said they knew a woman who was a victim of spousal abuse, but only 9% had actually talked with an abused woman. Although polling data continue to reveal some variation in the number of people who say they know someone who is a victim of spousal abuse (with reports ranging from 30% to 57% of respondents claiming they do), our surveys made clear that there was a marked division between knowledge and action: Two out of three Americans who said they knew a victim of domestic violence had nevertheless *failed to even talk to her about the abuse.*

The survey also revealed that levels of participation in domestic violence efforts were low compared with the public's engagement in other social issues that have been popularized over the years. In July 1994, only 18% of Lieberman poll respondents said they had done something about domestic violence in the previous year—but 56% had done something to help the environment and 43% had aided children living in poverty. Encouragingly, however, fully 40% of respondents also said they would like to do something to help reduce domestic violence in the coming year (see Table 6.1).

From Knowledge to Action

During 1994-1995, the general public showed a remarkable change in their view of and response to domestic violence. At unprecedented levels, women began

TABLE 6.1 Percentage of Respondents Who Took Action on Various Social Issues in the Previous Year

	July 1994 (N = 735)	January-February 1995[a] (N = 486)	November 1995 (N = 742)	January-February 1995 Versus November 1995
Domestic violence	18	21	24	+3
The environment	56	58	56	−2
Children living in poverty	43	49	47	−2
Street crime	18	18	20	+2
Teenage alcoholism	17	17	17	±0
Teenage pregnancy	14	19	20	+1
None	24	24	24	±0

SOURCE: These data are from polls conducted by Lieberman Research, Inc., working with the Family Violence Prevention Fund and The Advertising Council. For details see Appendix C.

a. The second wave of polling by Lieberman Research took place from November 1994 to February 1995. However, data from the shorter January-February period were used here so that they would be more comparable to the first- and third-wave polls, which were conducted in a single month.

to acknowledge publicly the violence in their lives—and their friends and relatives began to talk to them about the abuse as well. Whereas only 9% of Lieberman poll respondents had talked with an abused woman as of July 1994, 17% had done so by November 1995. This is a positive sign that this issue, which has been ignored and denied for centuries, is finally beginning to permeate public consciousness.

In addition to acknowledging the problem, Americans are increasingly grappling with the question of what to do about domestic violence. The Lieberman polling data show a small but steady increase in the number of people who have taken action to reduce domestic violence in the past year (especially among women, who showed a 6% increase in likelihood to do so between July 1994 and February 1995). In July 1994, 18% of respondents reported that they had done something within the previous year about domestic violence. By February 1995, that percentage had increased to 21%, and by November 1995, it had increased to 24% (see Table 6.2).

Women who themselves have been abused are significantly more likely to take action against abuse than the average American (52% vs. 24%), according to the Lieberman poll in November 1995. What's more, dramatic gains were made among certain groups between July 1994 and November 1995. Comparing results from Lieberman polls conducted both times, respondents in the more recent poll who themselves have faced abuse were much more likely to take

TABLE 6.2 Percentage of Respondents Who Took Action to Reduce Domestic
Violence in the Previous Year, Various Groups Compared

	July 1994	*November 1994-February 1995*	*November 1995*	*November 1994-February 1995 Versus November 1995*	*(Average Base)*
Total	18	20	24	+4[a]	(820)
California	20	19	23	+4	(229)
Those who know an abused woman	31	38	42	+4	(261)
Women who have been abused	31	31	52	+21[a]	(114)
Gender					
Female	19	25	30	+5	(412)
Male	17	16	18	+2	(408)
Age					
18 to 34	14	16	22	+6[a]	(333)
35 to 49 years	24	22	25	+3	(303)
50 to 65 years	19	25	28	+3	(176)
Household income					
< $20,000	21	18	29	+11[a]	(161)
$20,000 to $39,999	19	20	23	+3	(239)
$40,000 or more	19	23	25	+2	(303)
Type of area					
City	19	17	30	+13[a]	(210)
Suburban	18	21	22	+1	(278)
Small town/rural	18	21	22	+1	(329)

SOURCE: These data are from polls conducted by Lieberman Research, Inc., working with the Family
Violence Prevention Fund and The Advertising Council. For details see Appendix C.

a. Differences significant at a 95% confidence interval.

action (31% in 1994 vs. 52% in 1995). This increase in willingness to take action
among former victims was much larger than the corresponding increase during
the same time period among people who know victims (31% vs. 42%), 18- to
34-year-olds (14% vs. 22%), 50- to 65-year-olds (19% vs. 28%), those living in
lower-income households (21% vs. 29%), and city dwellers (19% vs. 30%).

The most common actions taken by Americans within the previous year to
help reduce domestic violence were discussing how to stop domestic violence
with friends and coworkers (done by 18% of the public) and talking directly
with a woman facing violence at home. There has been a steady and substantial
increase in the number of people who have talked with an abused woman directly
since July 1994 (9% vs. 17% in November 1995) (see Table 6.3).

TABLE 6.3 Percentage of Respondents Who Took Specific Actions to Reduce Domestic Violence

	July 1994 *(N = 735)*	*January-February 1995*[a] *(N = 486)*	*November 1995* *(N = 742)*	*January-February 1995 Versus November 1995*
Total who took action in previous year	18	21	24	+3
Talked to an abused woman	9	16	17	+1
Donated money	8	11	11	±0
Talked to an abusive man	6	8	11	+3
Did volunteer work	6	7	7	±0
Reduced domestic violence as part of job	3	5	7	+2
Called the police	2	5	3	−2
Offered abused women food, shelter, moral support	2	2	3	+1
Intervened in a fight	2	b	1	+1
Arranged/received professional support	2	1	1	±0
Discussed how to stop domestic violence with friends/coworkers	NA	NA	18	NA
Got involved with local programs that help reduce domestic violence	NA	NA	8	NA
Didn't take any action	82	79	76	−3

SOURCE: These data are from polls conducted by Lieberman Research, Inc., working with the Family Violence Prevention Fund and The Advertising Council. For details see Appendix C.

a. The second wave of polling by Lieberman Research took place from November 1994 to February 1995. However, data from the shorter January-February period were used here so that they would be more comparable to the first- and third-wave polls, which were conducted in a single month.

b. Less than 0.5 percent.

These results also confirm that although respondents to the 1992 EDK poll said they would be willing to do a number of things to address domestic violence—including donating money to a shelter and helping a woman facing abuse—these results were more indicative of the emerging social unacceptability of ignoring the problem (see Chapter 3). The Lieberman Research results indicate that as far as concrete action, Americans hadn't actually done much about domestic violence until relatively recently. The good news, however, is that things seem to be changing, albeit slowly. And what's more, we now have a better sense of why Americans *don't* get involved—reasons that can be addressed in future public education efforts on this subject.

With the public ready to take action against domestic violence, advocates and policymakers in the field must provide the public with some direction for action (after all, despite an increase in the number of people getting involved, fully

76% of respondents to the November 1995 Lieberman poll had *not* done anything about domestic violence in the previous year). Experts have paid little attention to the question of how to involve and engage the general citizenry in addressing the problem. Over the next decade, advocates must identify and promote simple, safe, and effective action steps that address three distinct levels: person-to-person contact, individual action, and community action.

Person-to-Person Contact

Individuals everywhere must be educated about how to talk effectively with and give support to women they know who are currently victims of abuse so that they can help real people living with or trying to escape from violent homes. One of the problems facing battered women is their sense of isolation and shame. Yet if advocates can help create a world in which battered women are surrounded by friends and relatives nonjudgmentally offering support, referrals, and resources, victims will have a much easier time finding the courage to leave and the help to make it happen.

Although such conversations are often emotionally difficult—and may require the commitment of the intervenor to have ongoing discussions with the victim about the situation—this kind of support is invaluable. Lieberman polls indicate that educating the public about how to engage in these conversations would be a good idea: Fully 38% of respondents in November 1995 felt they "wouldn't know what to say to an abused woman." Giving them a level of comfort with this kind of intervention might prompt more people to reach out—to both battered women and their children.

For centuries, the public has helped create what Secretary of Health and Human Services Donna Shalala has called "America's dirty little secret," turning a blind eye toward friends and coworkers who are batterers and failing to sanction the violent behavior. Social sanctions imposed by individuals who are close to the batterer—for example, withholding friendship, social status, or acceptance—are powerful ways to sway behavior. Thus friends and relatives of batterers—those who have pre-existing relationships based on love, affection, and understanding—are in a unique position to have a real impact on a batterer's behavior by addressing the violence directly and calling it unacceptable.

Although many programs have developed literature about how to talk with a victim about the abuse, few have applied the same principle to the batterer: developing materials about how to confront a friend, relative, or coworker who is a batterer to let him know that his behavior is unacceptable. Lieberman poll data suggest that this would be a good idea: 37% of respondents in November 1995 felt they "wouldn't know what to say to a man who was abusing a woman." Communicating, especially with men, about the importance of condemning violent behavior and providing them with some direction for how to have difficult confrontations in a way that does not further jeopardize the victim of abuse will help create an environment in which antiwomen violence becomes as socially unacceptable as racist violence or anti-Semitic violence.

Other behavior-change efforts have experimented successfully with the use of social sanctions and social support as effective ways to alter behavior. For example, an AIDS prevention study conducted in three gay bars in different cities demonstrated that safe sex practices endorsed by peers who were perceived by others as popular were likely to be adopted. These interventions consistently produced reductions in reported high-risk sexual behavior (Kelly et al., 1992). Similar studies must be designed and evaluated on the issue of domestic violence to explore the extent to which social sanctions (i.e., ostracism and loss of social status and affiliation) are effective in changing the behavior of batterers and the extent to which social support for victims encourages them to seek and receive help.

To develop effective social sanctions and messages, advocates must learn more about what currently *prevents* men from approaching and talking to men who batter and what messages batterers will respond to. Focus group tests that examine different messages with groups of potential intervenors and former batterers would be a useful way to help determine effective intervention strategies and messages.

Individual Action

One of the real challenges of the domestic violence community over the next couple of years must be to come up with ways for individuals to get involved with domestic violence in a relatively simple fashion that does not put them at risk—the domestic violence movement's equivalent of the drunk driving movement's "take the keys away." Action steps must be clearly articulated and promulgated to potential intervenors in a way that carefully avoids any endorsement of direct physical intervention, which could put individuals at risk, dissuading people from getting involved. Because there is a large continuum in terms of people's willingness to get involved, many different action steps must be promulgated to appeal to people at every level of commitment.

The Family Violence Prevention Fund's *There's No Excuse for Domestic Violence* public education campaign includes a national toll-free number (1-800-END-ABUSE), publicized in each of the campaign's PSAs, which provides free Action Kits to callers. The action steps promoted in this kit were developed from Lieberman polling results indicating what respondents said they would be most likely to do to address the issue of domestic violence (see Table 6.4).

Respondents to the November 1995 Lieberman poll said they would be willing to take a variety of different steps to address domestic violence, when it was made clear that those steps could be taken safely. For example, 70% said

TABLE 6.4 Actions Respondents Would Be Most Willing to Take to Help Reduce Domestic Violence (by percent)

	Willing to Do This	First Choice	Second Choice	Third Choice	Among Top Three
If driving in a car and you see a man hitting a woman, try to draw public attention by honking the horn loudly and repeatedly	85	27	16	15	58
Ask clergy to talk about domestic violence in a sermon	70	10	14	9	33
Call/write to elected officials to ask them to do more about domestic violence	67	12	9	12	33
Wear T-shirts or buttons that say "There's no excuse for domestic violence"	64	15	15	12	42
Put a bumper sticker on your car or in the window of your house that says "There's no excuse for domestic violence"	61	13	14	11	38
Distribute information at work about domestic violence	56	9	7	7	23
Contact local television/radio stations to ask them to run public service announcements about domestic violence	55	5	11	9	25
Contact local newspaper/television/radio stations to complain if you see or hear news story that minimizes problem of domestic violence	54	5	7	7	19

SOURCE: These data are from a poll conducted in November 1995 by Lieberman Research, Inc., working with the Family Violence Prevention Fund and The Advertising Council. For details see Appendix C.

NOTE: Respondents were first asked whether they would be willing to take each action; then they were asked if it would be their first choice, second choice, or third choice.

they would be willing to ask clergy to talk about domestic violence in a sermon, and 64% said they would be willing to wear a T-shirt or buttons with anti-domestic violence messages on them. More surprising was that a majority of respondents said they would be willing to take other, more committed actions such as distributing information at work (56%), calling or writing to elected officials to ask them to do more about domestic violence (67%), and contacting local television or radio stations to ask them to run PSAs about domestic violence (54%).

This is very good news. These results indicate a high level of willingness on the part of individuals across the country to engage in time-consuming activities related to domestic violence prevention. Public education campaigns on this issue can capitalize on the current threshold for action by promoting the very specific things they would like Americans to do about this devastating problem.

Community Action

Every successful social change movement requires the commitment not only of individuals but also of entire communities. Orchestrated, community-wide actions and demonstrations have a powerful ability to sway public opinion, attract media support and resources, and keep community-based institutions accountable.

The AIDS movement has been particularly successful in some areas of the country at galvanizing public support and funneling community energies into a collective project. In San Francisco, the city's annual AIDS March serves as a moving reminder every year of the thousands of people who have died since the epidemic began, raising awareness about the problem and its massive effects on the lives of real people, and giving activists the opportunity to lobby publicly for increased aid for services, prevention, and other policy changes. In cities where the Names Project's traveling AIDS quilt is exhibited—each of the many thousands of panels that compose it representing a victim of AIDS who has died—the enormous display serves the same purpose, allowing every individual to participate in the AIDS movement.

The domestic violence movement must create a similar kind of public event that invites mass participation, involving all members of the community in recognizing, remembering, and mourning victims, raising awareness about the issue, and holding institutions to which battered women turn accountable for their response. Just as Mothers Against Drunk Driving instituted court monitoring to gauge the way judges handled individual drunk driving cases, activists could pack courtrooms in which domestic violence cases are being decided and report poorly handled incidents to the press. And just as the Ms. Foundation's "Take Our Daughters to Work Day" encouraged business communities across the country to welcome the future female workforce and give young girls a vision of possible career paths, the domestic violence movement must create a day on which the media and business communities come together to condemn abusive behavior and show young girls and boys that there is another way of life. Advocates must determine the most effective forum for such public events and begin working to make them happen.

In addition, community organizers and elected officials who might be persuaded to take this issue on must be provided with successful model programs that are tailored to raise awareness about the problem and help change behavior at workplaces, in schools, and in neighborhoods around the country. Such projects are beginning to emerge all over the United States. For example, the Minnesota Coalition for Battered Women has launched a statewide initiative called *Hands Are Not for Hitting,* an effort to educate young schoolchildren about nonviolence. The Taylor Institute in Chicago is working in a low-income community to begin a schoolwide conversation and educational process about domestic violence. And in a good example of corporate investment in domestic violence prevention, Marshalls, Inc., has raised money to create an awards program called *Marshalls' Domestic Peace Prize,* which annually identifies and recognizes model and replicable grassroots prevention programs that are helping to reduce and end domestic violence. The first awards were made in October 1995.

At the United Nations Fourth World Conference on Women, which took place in September 1995, the Family Violence Prevention Fund sponsored a program to help identify original community-based models from around the globe. This workshop, called *From Private Problem to Community Concern: Preventing Domestic Violence Before It Begins,* brought together presenters from all over the world who are engaged in innovative community-based prevention strategies, serving as an excellent opportunity to learn first-hand of the pioneering approaches of activist women from around the globe (many of whom have had to rely on community-based action in the face of reluctant law enforcement response to the problem). This forum was an excellent opportunity to learn about new models for community involvement.

More of these model programs must be identified and funded. These new ideas must be disseminated to grassroots communities to be replicated. Information vehicles must be used to carry word of effective new approaches and must be expanded beyond the domestic violence community: PTAs, men's groups, youth groups, community health clinics, and so on, must be included in providing and promoting community-based responses to violence.

Expanding the constituency of people concerned about and active in addressing domestic violence is critical. Spokespeople for the issue must include leaders from the legal, justice, health, education, entertainment, sports, media, political, corporate, and civil rights fields, as well as representatives from the women's and domestic violence communities. Developing leadership among men is particularly important, as it will help position domestic violence as a universal problem, not exclusively a women's issue. It will also help convey the message that not *all* men batter women—but that *too many* do, and that men can be responsible for helping to reduce those numbers. In addition, men speaking out against domestic violence—particularly men drawn from the sports, civil rights, and entertainment arenas—will provide new role models for young boys, creating an environment in which beating girls and women is never socially acceptable or "cool."

Already, such men's groups are beginning to emerge—at Morehouse College in Atlanta, a group called Black Men for the Eradication of Sexism was formed to respond to misogyny on campus, and at Northeastern University in Boston, an organization called Sports in Society trains male athletes to speak out against violence against women. Male leaders from the political arena to the pop music industry are beginning to speak out as well. President Bill Clinton, who knows the effects of domestic violence first-hand after having watched his mother suffer from it for many years, has challenged all men to take a pledge against ever raising a hand against a woman in violence, and Louis Farrakhan voiced similar themes at the Million Man March.

Encouraging spokespeople from many different fields to speak out against domestic violence will create an environment in which victims know that they are not alone and that there is help available, and in which batterers begin to recognize that their behavior will increasingly carry negative consequences. Already, such a shift has begun. On *Court TV*, which covered the Simpson trial most closely, Robert Honecker, Jr., second assistant prosecutor of Monmouth, New Jersey, appeared and commented that

> This type of activity should not be condoned. . . . If you are aware of this type of situation, by not speaking out, you in fact condone it—and something as horrendous as a death may result. So it is important that if you are aware of it, come and speak out about it.

More and more, this changed environment encourages survivors to come forward to tell their stories, increasing both public awareness about the issue and public commitment to ending the epidemic. When *Time* printed a photograph capturing a domestic violence situation taken by Donna Ferrato, Connie Galiazzo DeJuliis, a state delegate from Maryland, saw the photo and decided to admit publicly that she herself had once been a victim of domestic violence. Testifying on June 30, 1994, at a congressional subcommittee hearing, she said,

> This is the first time I've made any public statement about this issue. I'm here today because of a picture in *Time* magazine. It showed an 8-year-old boy. With his finger pointing at his father, he said, "I hate you for beating my mother." Another picture flashed in my mind; I saw another little boy. He was almost 7 years old. His mother saw his face peering over a bannister as his father brutally beat her, and she told him, "Go to your room." I am that mother. That day, a little over 25 years ago, I took my children and I walked out.

The statement appeared in the national evening news around the country.

Now is the time to promote action. The *Time*/CNN poll on January 11 and 12, 1995, found that only 3% of Americans said domestic violence is *not* a serious problem in our society right now. Advocates and government officials alike must seize the day with ways to galvanize the American public to address this costly and devastating epidemic. The action steps that are developed today will help address abuse and aid battered women long after the public spotlight has shifted.

Appendix A
EDK Focus Groups

Methodology

Prior to this study, there was no comprehensive, national study of public knowledge or concern about domestic violence. To determine the public's understanding and knowledge about violence against women, the Family Violence Prevention Fund, funded by a grant from the Ford Foundation, hired EDK Associates, a New York-based public opinion research firm, to conduct both qualitative and quantitative research on public attitudes toward domestic violence. The overall study was designed by Ethel Klein, President of EDK Associates, and James Robinson, President of Robinson and Muenster Associates. They were assisted by Esta Soler, Executive Director of the Family Violence Prevention Fund; June Zeitlin, Program Director of the Ford Foundation; Joanne Howes, Vice President of Bass & Howes; and the Ford Foundation Advisory Committee.

Focus Groups

Focus groups, a research technique based on bringing about 10 people into a room to have a conversation about an issue, were assembled to explore the texture, language, and psychological context that men and women bring to the issue of domestic violence. The study was designed to reach a broad cross-section of the population from differing education levels and ethnic backgrounds. The participants were told they were coming to participate in a 2-hour discussion about relationships between men and women. They were not selected on the basis of their exposure to or knowledge of domestic violence—nor did they know that they would be talking about this issue prior to its being introduced during the groups. Participants were recruited by market research companies in each city according to the specifications below. Participants were paid between $35 and $50 for their time.

The demographic profile of the groups was as follows:

- Three groups of *white women* (two in Hartford, CT, and one in Little Rock, AR). In two of the groups, the participants had no more than a high school diploma (about a third in each group had not completed high school). In the third group, all had at least some college education (almost half were college graduates).

- Two groups of *white men* (one in Little Rock, AR, and one in Dallas, TX). In Little Rock, the men had no more than a high school diploma (60% did not graduate from high school), and in Dallas, all the participants had at least some college education (50% were college graduates). The groups were facilitated by a white, male moderator.

- Three groups of *African Americans* (one group of women in Dallas, a women's group in Los Angeles, and a men's group in Los Angeles). In Dallas, the women had at least some college education (50% were college graduates). In Los Angeles, participants in both the men's and women's groups had not graduated from the college. The women's groups were facilitated by an African American woman moderator. The men's group was facilitated by an African American man moderator.

- Two groups of *Latinos* (one group of men, one of women, both in Los Angeles). Participants in both groups had not graduated from college. At least a third of each group were not born in the United States but were raised here. The Latinas group was conducted in Spanish by a Latina moderator. The Latino group was conducted in Spanish and English by a Latino moderator.

- Two groups of Asian Americans (one consisted of men, another of women, both in San Francisco, CA). In both groups, the education level ranged from high school to college graduates.

The groups were conducted between January 20 and January 29, 1992. Each group included an average of 10 participants.

Focus Group Question Guide: Women

I. Warm-up

Tell me something about yourself—your family, your work, the things you like to do.

What worries you these days?

What is the biggest problem facing women today?

What is going well in your life? (What is making you happy?)

II. Setting the Context From the Participant's Perspective

Do you think men understand women? Do you think they like women? Do you think women like men?

Think about the men you know in your family and where you work. Do most of them respect women?

Finish this sentence:

- The thing that drives me crazy about men is . . .
- When my husband/boyfriend gets angry, he . . .
- When my husband/boyfriend gets angry, I . . .

Are women really the weaker sex? [After respondents answer, direct the conversation to whether they are threatened by men's greater strength.]

Do men take advantage of the fact they are physically stronger?

Have you ever been frightened that a man might hit you? Rape you?

Word Association

women

men

home

victim

sex roles

violence

power

If I told you I met a man who was beaten up, how would you guess this happened? Who did it? Why?

If I told you I met a woman who was beaten up, how would you guess this happened? Who did it? Why?

Suppose she was beaten up by her boyfriend. What do you think happened? Tell me something about this woman, about who you think she might be. [Probe for race, ethnicity, age, class, etc., if they don't respond.] What should she do?

What about the man? What can you tell me about him? Why did he do it? What should happen to him?

What if she was beaten up by her husband? What do you think happened? What should she do?

Do any of you know of anyone who has been beaten up by her boyfriend or husband?

When you were a teenager, did your date or one of your girlfriend's dates ever lose his temper and get violent? [Probe "What happened—what did he do? What did she do? What did he do after the date? What happened to him? What kind of husband do you think he would make? The goal here is to extend the definition of domestic violence beyond married couples.]

Why do men beat women? [Pursue—Don't women ask for it? Push men beyond limits? Then probe for family reasons, alcohol, television/ movies, what we teach boys and girls.]

Can anything be done?

What would you do if your neighbor were beaten? [Probe why most people would do nothing.]

What would you do if your daughter were beaten?

Have you and your husband/boyfriend ever discussed this subject? Are you or would you be comfortable talking to him about this? What does or would he say?

III. Setting the Context From Our Perspective

How serious is this problem of women being beaten? Is it fairly common or pretty rare? Take a guess at how many Americans are affected by this form of violence each year. [After discussion, get response to the actual figures.]

What if I were to tell you that:

- One third of the murders between family members involved wives killing their husbands; two thirds involved husbands killing their wives.
- More women are injured or killed from being beaten than in car accidents, muggings, and rapes combined. [4,000 women are beaten to death annually.]
- Every year violence between family members affects more than 2.1 million women, 4 million children, and 1 million elderly.

What if I were to tell you that:

- One third of all women who go to hospital emergency rooms are women who have been beaten by their husbands or boyfriends.
- One out of four women who attempt suicide have had a history of being beaten.

What about children? What happens to them? [See if they can distinguish between domestic violence and child abuse; do they become more involved or more comfortable when the focus shifts to children?]

What if I were to tell you:

- Beatings during pregnancy are the single largest cause of birth defects today.
- Juvenile delinquents are four times more likely to come from homes in which their fathers beat their mothers.
- Children who witness their mothers being beaten are five times more likely to become batterers or victims.

Suppose you were watching a talk show on women who have been beaten by their husbands or boyfriends and a guest made the following statement. Please tell me if you agree with the statement, disagree, or don't really understand what the person is trying to say. Tell me who you think made the statement (what kind of person).

[Moderator hands out statements and gets participants to rank each statement on a scale of 0 (Hate it) to 10 (Completely agree). Also ask them to underline what they like and circle what they do not like.]

- Beating up on women is often learned in the home. Some people learn to be violent because, when they were young, they were beaten or witnessed violence in their home. Many people think violence is the only way to solve their problems.
- Men who assault their wives are actually living up to cultural perceptions that are encouraged by our society—aggressiveness, male dominance, and female subordination—and they are using physical force to enforce that dominance.
- Violence against women robs women of self-confidence, hope, and self-esteem. It is more than a physical assault; it is an attack on a woman's dignity and freedom.
- Each act of violence against a single woman intimidates and terrifies all women.

- As long as women are economically dependent on men, they will always be potential victims of violence.
- As long as women are emotionally dependent on men, they will always be potential victims of violence.

IV. Solutions

Now let me tell you about some things that can be done to help stop men from beating women. Tell me what you think of the following as potential solutions to the problem.

- Early intervention—encouraging the arrest and punishment of teenage boys who abuse their girlfriends
- Mandatory arrests
- Civil suits against the abuser [Moderator defines civil suits]
- Laws requiring hospitals to identify and report incidents
- Mandatory 48 hours of confinement to separate victim from abuser
- Mandatory treatment of abuser
- Reduce the amount of violence on television [After response, probe if this is realistic.]
- Education courses for young boys and girls about sex roles and how to resolve conflict (at what age?)
- Getting more money into the criminal justice system to prosecute offenders
- Getting more money into shelters to help battered women

V. Message Testing I: The Facts That Move People

Statistics

I am going to hand out a list of statistics about women being beaten. Read the list with me and then mark down the four statistics that you think are most effective in getting people to think about this problem.

- One out of three deaths in murders between family members involves a man who has been killed by his wife.
- More women are injured or killed by being beaten than in car accidents, muggings, and rapes combined.
- Every 15 seconds, a woman is beaten by her husband or boyfriend.

- Every 15 seconds, a woman is beaten by her husband or boyfriend.
- Over half of the women murdered in this country every year are killed by their partners or ex-partners.
- Beating pregnant women is the single largest cause of birth defects today.
- Juvenile delinquents are four times more likely to come from homes in which their fathers beat their mothers.
- One third of all women who go to the emergency room have been beaten by their husbands or boyfriends.

VI. Message Testing II: Designing the Campaign

Suppose a company hired us to figure out how to get people to understand this problem better and to take the problem of women being beaten seriously.

What would we call the problem of men beating women? [If they say wife abuse, remind them that many women are beaten by their boyfriends.]

What would we call the project?

Slogans

If we had to come up with a slogan for this campaign, what would it be?

- The home is the most dangerous place for women.
- _____ does not go away on its own. [Put whatever name the group decides to label the problem in the blank]
- _____—the single greatest health threat to women.

Slides

Show some slides and get their response.

Video

Show some video and get their response.

VII. Conclusion: What Would You Be Willing to Do?

You have been really great and we are about to wrap up now, but I would like to ask something about what you can do. I know all of you are busy and don't have a lot of time or money, but what would you be willing to do about this? If there are many other important problems people face. If you think that this is an important issue, but you are more concerned about other things, please tell me that as well.

So what would you do?

[After open-ended discussion, close by saying] OK, just to get this straight, please raise your hand if you are willing to do any of the following:

- Nothing
- Give money to an organization that is trying to end this violence
- Work in a shelter
- Lobby your state representative or congressperson
- Talk about this to your friends
- Talk about this with your husband or boyfriend

Focus Group Question Guide: Men

I. Warm-up

Tell me something about yourself—your family, your work, the things you like to do.

What worries you these days?

What is the biggest problem facing men today?

What is going well in your life? (What is making you happy?)

II. Setting the Context From the Participant's Perspective

Do you think women understand men? Do you think they like men?

Do you think men like women?

Think about the men you know in your family and where you work. Do most of them respect women?

Let me read to you some things men have said to me and tell me if you feel this way or not:

- It drives me crazy when women cry to get their way.
- Women are too emotional, I wish they were more logical.
- Men are smarter than women.
- My wife/girlfriend expects too much from me.

- Women can nag you to death.
- I wish women were more like men. [Probe what that would mean.]
- I hate it when my wife/girlfriend tries to manipulate me.

Finish this sentence:

- The thing that drives me crazy about women is . . .
- When my wife/girlfriend gets angry, she . . .
- When my wife/girlfriend gets angry, I . . .

Are women really the weaker sex? [After respondents answer, direct the conversation to whether they think women are threatened by men's greater strength.]
Do women take advantage of the fact that they are physically weaker?
Do men take advantage of the fact that they are physically stronger?

Word Association

women
men
home
victim
sex roles
violence
power

If I told you I met a man who was beaten up, how would you guess this happened? Who did it? Why?
If I told you I met a woman who was beaten up, how would you guess this happened? Who did it? Why?
Suppose she was beaten up by her boyfriend. What do you think happened? Tell me something about this woman, about who you think she might be. [Probe for race, ethnicity, age, class, etc., if they don't respond.] What should she do?
What about the man? What can you tell me about him? Why did he do it? What should happen to him?
What if she was beaten up by her husband? What do you think happened? What should she do?

Do any of you know of any woman who has been beaten up by her boyfriend or husband?

Do any of you know of any man who has been attacked by his wife or girlfriend?

Why do men beat their women? [Pursue: Don't women ask for it? Push men beyond limits? Then probe for family reasons, alcohol, television/movies, what we teach boys and girls.]

Can anything be done?

What would you do if your neighbor were beaten? [Probe why most people would do nothing.]

What would you do if your daughter were beaten?

Have you and your wife/girlfriend ever discussed this subject? Are you or would you be comfortable talking to her about this? What does or would she say?

III. Setting the Context From Our Perspective

How serious is this problem of violence between men and women? Is it fairly common or pretty rare? Is it dangerous for men as well as for women? Take a guess at how many men are affected by this form of violence each year. How many women are victims of beatings?

[After discussion get response to the actual figures.]

What if I were to tell you that:

- One third of the murders between family members involved wives killing their husbands; two thirds involved husbands killing wives.
- More women are injured or killed from being beaten than in car accidents, muggings, and rapes combined. [4,000 women are beaten to death annually]
- Every year violence between family members affects more than 2.1 million women, 4 million children, and 1 million elderly.

What about the children? What happens to them? [See if they can distinguish between domestic violence and child abuse; do they become more involved or more comfortable when the focus shifts to children?]

What if I were to tell you:

- Beatings during pregnancy are the single-largest cause of birth defects today.
- Juvenile delinquents are four times more likely to come from homes in which their fathers beat their mothers.

- Children who witness their mothers being beaten are five times more likely to become batterers or victims.

Suppose you were watching a talk show on women who have been beaten by their husbands or boyfriends and a guest made the following statement. Please tell me if you agree with the statement, disagree, or don't really understand what the person is trying to say. Tell me who you think made the statement (what kind of person).

[Moderator hands out statements and gets participants to rank each statement on a scale of 0 (Hate it) to 10 (Completely agree). Also ask them to underline what they like and circle what they do not like.]

- Beating up on women is often learned in the home. Some people learn to be violent because, when they were young, they were beaten or witnessed violence in their home. Many people think violence is the only way to solve their problems.
- Men who assault their wives are actually living up to cultural perceptions that are encouraged by our society—aggressiveness, male dominance, and female subordination—and they are using physical force to enforce that dominance.
- Violence against women robs women of self-confidence, hope, and self-esteem. It is more than a physical assault, it is an attack on a woman's dignity and freedom.
- Each act of violence against a single woman intimidates and terrifies all women.
- As long as women are economically dependent on men, they will always be potential victims of violence.

IV. Solutions

Now let me tell you about some things that can be done to help stop men from beating women. Tell me what you think of the following as potential solutions to the problem.

- Early intervention—encouraging the arrest and punishment of teenage boys who abuse their girlfriends
- Mandatory arrests
- Civil suits against the abuser [Moderator defines civil suit.]
- Laws requiring hospitals to identify and report incidents
- Mandatory 48 hours of confinement to separate victim from abuser

- Mandatory treatment of abuser
- Reduce the amount of violence on television [After response, probe if this is realistic.]
- Education courses for young boys and girls about sex roles and how to resolve conflict (at what age?)
- Getting more money into the criminal justice system to prosecute offenders
- Getting more emergency money into shelters to help battered women

V. Message Testing I: The Facts That Move People

Statistics

I am going to hand out a list of statistics about women being beaten. Read the list with me and then mark down the four statistics that you think are most effective in getting people to think about this problem.

- One out of three deaths in murders between family members involved a man who has been killed by his wife.
- More women are injured or killed by being beaten than in car accidents, muggings, and rapes combined.
- Every 15 seconds a woman is beaten by her husband or boyfriend.
- Over half of the women murdered in this country every year are killed by their partners or ex-partners.
- Beating pregnant women is the single largest cause of birth defects today.
- Juvenile delinquents are four times more likely to come from homes in which their fathers beat their mothers.
- One third of all women who go to the emergency room have been beaten by their husbands or boyfriends.

VI. Message Testing II: Designing the Campaign

Suppose a company hired us to figure out how to get people to understand this problem better and to take the problem of women being beaten seriously.

What would we call the problem of men beating women. [If they say wife abuse, remind them that many women are beaten by their boyfriends.]

What would we call the project?

Slogans

If we had to come up with a slogan for this campaign, what would it be?

- The home is the most dangerous place for women.
- _____ does not go away on its own. [Put whatever name the group decides to label the problem in the blank]
- _____—the single greatest health threat to women.

Slides

[Show some slides and get their response.]

Video

[Show some video and get their response.]

VII. Conclusion: What Would You Be Willing to Do?

You have been really great and we are about to wrap up now, but I would like to ask something about what you can do. I know all of you are busy and don't have a lot of time or money, but what would you be willing to do about this. If you feel that you can't do anything please tell me, I want to know that. Also, there are many other important problems people face. If you think that this is an important issue, but you are more concerned about other things, please tell me that as well.

So what would you do?

[After open-ended discussion close by saying] OK, just to get this straight, please raise your hand if you are willing to do any of the following:

- Nothing
- Give money to an organization that is trying to end this violence
- Work in a shelter
- Lobby your state representative or Congressperson
- Talk about this to your friends
- Talk about this with your wife or girlfriend

Appendix B

EDK Opinion Survey of Public Attitudes
Toward Domestic Violence

Methodology

The information from the unstructured focus groups was translated into a series of structured questions to determine if the findings were representative of the general population. The Family Violence Prevention Fund Opinion Survey on Public Attitudes Toward Domestic Violence is the most comprehensive survey on this issue to be conducted to date. The survey was conducted by EDK Associates, a New York-based research firm, between April 15 and 26, 1992. The national sample was purchased from Survey Sampling, located in Connecticut. The phone numbers were randomly selected within the sample in replicate order. When no contact was made, the phone number was called a total of four different days and times before being withdrawn from the sample. The telephone interviews were completed with 1,000 men and women age 18 and older, reflecting the racial composition of the overall U.S. population. The margin of error is 3%.

In order to conduct an in-depth demographic analysis and comparison across sex, race, and ethnicity, EDK Associates conducted three additional, slightly shortened surveys, oversampling 300 African Americans, 300 Latinos, and 300 Asian Americans, using samples compiled to targeted specific segments of the population. These telephone surveys were conducted from May 15 through May 22, 1992. The Latino interviewers were bilingual, and most of the surveys were conducted in Spanish. The African American surveys were conducted by African American interviewers. The Asian American surveys were conducted largely by Asian American interviewers.

Survey Instrument and Polling Results

Domestic Violence Poll Conducted by EDK Associates

(Questions 1-6)
People worry about different things.
Are you very worried, worried, or not worried about the following:

1. Crime and drugs

42%	Very worried
48%	Worried
9%	Not worried

2. Pollution and environmental problems

37%	Very worried
50%	Worried
12%	Not worried

3. The growth in family violence

34%	Very worried
44%	Worried
20%	Not worried
1%	Don't know

4. Health care

43%	Very worried
43%	Worried
14%	Not worried

5. Day care

12%	Very worried
34%	Worried
50%	Not worried
3%	Don't know

6. AIDS

53%	Very worried
33%	Worried
13%	Not worried
1%	Don't know

(Questions 7-22)
Have you ever witnessed any of the
following forms of violence?

7. Have you ever witnessed a robbery or a mugging?

10%	Yes, robbery
4%	Yes, mugging
4%	Yes, both
81%	No

8. [If yes] Have you been robbed or mugged?
   [Of 18% who said yes]

40%	Yes, robbed
11%	Yes, mugged
9%	Yes, both
40%	No

9. Have you ever witnessed people yelling loudly at one another and threatening to get violent?

57%	Yes
43%	No

10. [If yes] Were you ever in such a screaming match?
    [Of 57% who said yes]

35%	Yes
63%	No
2%	Don't know

11. Did you worry about the other person becoming violent?
    [Of 57% who said yes]

80%	Yes
18%	No
1%	Don't know

12. How about yourself—did you worry that you might get violent?
    [Of 57% who said yes]

52%	Yes
46%	No
1%	Don't know

13. Have you ever witnessed a parent beating a child?

3%	Yes
77%	No

14. [If yes] Were you or any of your brothers or sisters beaten as a child? [Of 3% who said yes]

33%	Yes
66%	No
1%	Don't know

15. Have you ever witnessed a man beating his wife or his girlfriend?

34%	Yes
65%	No

16. [If yes] Has a husband or boyfriend ever beaten your mother or step-mother? [Of 34% who said yes]

19%	Yes
79%	No
2%	Don't know

17. [If female who said yes to Question 16] Has a husband or boyfriend ever been violent with you? [Of subgroup]

41%	Yes
54%	No
5%	Don't know

18. [If yes] What did he do? [Do not read][1]

15%	Pushed me around hard
35%	Smacked me in the face
29%	Punched me
8%	Threatened to hurt me
3%	Choked me
9%	Kicked, scratched, bit me

19. Have you ever witnessed a woman beating her husband or boyfriend?

15%	Yes
84%	No

20. [If yes and male] Has a wife or girlfriend ever been violent to you?
    [Of subgroup]

    34%   Yes
    64%   No
    2%   Don't know

21. [If yes] What did she do? [Do not read]
    [Of subgroup]

    3%   Pushed me around hard
    34%   Smacked me in the face
    29%   Punched me
    6%   Shoved me
    9%   Threw things at me
    14%   Threatened to hurt me
    6%   Kicked, scratched, bit me

22. Do you think women being beaten by their husbands or boyfriends is a
    serious problem facing many families?

    87%   Yes
    6%   No
    7%   Don't know

(Questions 23-30)
Would you do any of the following to help reduce
the amount of violence against women?

23. If you know someone who was being beaten, would you talk to your
    friends, family, or clergy to try to figure out how to help this person?

    93%   Yes
    5%   No
    2%   Don't know

24. Would you tell the person to stop?

    79%   Yes
    12%   No
    9%   Don't know

25. Would you call the police if you saw a man beating his wife or girlfriend?

    90%   Yes
    5%   No
    5%   Don't know

26. Would you support legislation to increase funding for battered women's programs?

87%	Yes
6%	No
7%	Don't know

27. Would you give money to an organization working on this issue?

69%	Yes
18%	No
13%	Don't know

28. Would you volunteer some time and work in a program for battered women?

48%	Yes
39%	No
13%	Don't know

29. Do men often take advantage of the fact that they are physically stronger than women?

78%	Yes
13%	No
9%	Don't know

30. Do women often take advantage of the fact that they are physically weaker?

63%	Yes
23%	No
14%	Don't know

(Questions 31-41)
Let me read you some things people have said
and tell me if you agree or disagree.

[If agree/disagree ask] Is that strongly or not so strongly agree/disagree?

31. Women often cry to get their way.

20%	Strongly agree
39%	Not so strongly agree
24%	Not so strongly disagree
14%	Strongly disagree
4%	Don't know

32. Men think they can solve everything by yelling.

18%	Strongly agree
25%	Not so strongly agree
33%	Not so strongly disagree
20%	Strongly disagree
3%	Don't know

33. Men need to learn how to express themselves.

61%	Strongly agree
29%	Not so strongly agree
6%	Not so strongly disagree
3%	Strongly disagree
2%	Don't know

34. Women are too emotional.

21%	Strongly agree
33%	Not so strongly agree
28%	Not so strongly disagree
15%	Strongly disagree
3%	Don't know

35. Women expect too much from men.

17%	Strongly agree
27%	Not so strongly agree
33%	Not so strongly disagree
19%	Strongly disagree
4%	Don't know

36. Men expect too much from women.

30%	Strongly agree
32%	Not so strongly agree
24%	Not so strongly disagree
10%	Strongly disagree
4%	Don't know

37. Men often want to be in control.

59%	Strongly agree
29%	Not so strongly agree
6%	Not so strongly disagree

3%	Strongly disagree
2%	Don't know

38. Women often want a man to take care of them.

39%	Strongly agree
39%	Not so strongly agree
15%	Not so strongly disagree
5%	Strongly disagree
2%	Don't know

39. If you were eating in a nonsmoking section in a restaurant and someone was smoking, would you ask that person or get the waiter to ask that person to stop smoking?

57%	Yes
39%	No
3%	Don't know

40. If you were at a party and a friend of yours had too much to drink, would you ask him or her for the car keys and insist on driving your friend home?

95%	Yes
2%	No
2%	Don't know

41. If a friend of yours complained about his wife screaming and hitting him to the point where he said he had to slap her to calm her down, would you tell him that he should have walked away rather than hit her?

83%	Yes
9%	No
8%	Don't know

Let me read you some statements about some common situations. Please tell me what you would do in each case.

42. You are shopping at a mall and you pass a mother screaming and calling her child names. What would you do? [Do not read]

46%	Keep on walking
9%	Stare at her
30%	Intervene and ask her to stop
4%	Get help/call security
10%	Don't know

43. Is this child abuse?
    64%   Yes
    24%   No
    11%   Don't know

44. Should the child be removed from the home?
     6%   Yes
    69%   No
    26%   Don't know

45. You are shopping at a mall and you pass a mother hitting her child hard
    across his or her face and head. What would you do? [Do not read]
     8%   Keep on walking
     3%   Stare at her
    57%   Intervene and ask her to stop
    25%   Get help/call security
     7%   Don't know

46. Is this child abuse?
    92%   Yes
     3%   No
     4%   Don't know

47. Should the child be removed from the home?
    40%   Yes
    25%   No
    35%   Don't know

48. You are at a large family dinner and your cousin is fighting with his wife.
    He shoves her and smacks her across the face. What do you do? [Do not
    read]
     3%   Ignore them
     1%   Stare at him
    47%   Tell him to stop
    33%   Pull him aside and tell him that's no way to behave
     4%   Call police
     5%   I would have to hit him
     7%   Don't know

49. Is this domestic violence?

90%	Yes
5%	No
5%	Don't know

50. Should he be arrested?

29%	Yes
35%	No
17%	Up to wife
19%	Don't know

51. Should she leave him?

35%	Yes
29%	No
35%	Don't know

52. Suppose your neighbors were having another huge fight, screaming at each other at the top of their lungs. What would you do? [Do not read]

10%	Ignore it
35%	Call them and tell them to shut up
42%	Call the police
1%	Speak to him about it later
1%	Speak to her about it later
5%	Speak to both of them about it later
1%	Bang on the wall
6%	Don't know

53. Is this domestic violence?

53%	Yes
34%	No
13%	Don't know

54. Should he be arrested?

10%	Yes
63%	No
9%	Up to wife
17%	Don't know

55. Should she leave him?

    15%   Yes
    49%   No
    36%   Don't know

56. Suppose your neighbors were having a huge fight and you knew she was being beaten. What would you do? [Do not read]

    2%   Ignore it
    4%   Call them, tell them to stop
    84%   Call the police
    1%   Speak to him about it later
    2%   Speak to her about it later
    2%   Help her leave
    1%   Speak to both of them about it later
    3%   Don't know

57. Is this domestic violence?

    98%   Yes
    1%   No
    1%   Don't know

58. Should he be arrested?

    75%   Yes
    5%   No
    12%   Up to wife
    8%   Don't know

59. Should she leave him?

    62%   Yes
    7%   No
    31%   Don't know

60. Your daughter calls you after she and her husband or boyfriend had a big fight where he grabbed her by the blouse and called her a worthless cow. What would you do? [Do not read]

    21%   Talk to him
    19%   Talk to her
    18%   Suggest she leave
    16%   Go take her out of there immediately
    4%   Just listen and tell her you love her

5%	Tell her he will do it again/warn her this does not stop
5%	Nothing
1%	Call the police
1%	Talk to both of them
1%	Don't know

61. Is this domestic violence?

59%	Yes
30%	No
11%	Don't know

62. Should he be arrested?

15%	Yes
64%	No
9%	Up to wife
12%	Don't know

63. Should she leave him?

41%	Yes
33%	No
26%	Don't know

64. Your daughter calls you after she and her husband or boyfriend get into a big fight where he calls her a tramp and punches her in the face. What would you do? [Do not read]

8%	Talk to him
5%	Talk to her
16%	Suggest she leave
36%	Go take her out of there immediately
14%	Go and beat him
11%	Call the police
1%	Just listen and tell her you love her
1%	Nothing
7%	Talk to both of them
1%	Don't know

65. Is this domestic violence?

95%	Yes
3%	No
2%	Don't know

66. Should he be arrested?

69%	Yes
11%	No
11%	Up to wife
9%	Don't know

67. Should she leave him?

72%	Yes
8%	No
19%	Don't know

68. Suppose I told you a woman you knew was beaten up by her husband or boyfriend. Why do you think he did it? [Do not read]

5%	Woman provoked it by yelling/screaming/hitting him
14%	Probably drunk—didn't know what he was doing
12%	Didn't know how to communicate/couldn't control feelings
5%	Saw it at home when he was growing up
9%	Did it to control her/keep her in line/get her to do what he wants
—^{2}	To get her to listen or calm down
10%	Has bad self-esteem and is taking it out on her
7%	She cheated on him
9%	He is sick/disturbed/violent
29%	Don't know

69. Why do women stay in these relationships? [Do not read]

15%	Low self-esteem/think it's their fault
15%	Financially dependent
11%	Really love the guy
9%	Emotionally dependent
6%	Don't want family to break up/for sake of children
22%	She is afraid to leave
2%	Like it
5%	Grew up with it/don't know anything else
—	Religion
16%	Don't know

70. If your best friend or a relative was abused, where would you send her?

13%	Clergy
6%	Therapist/Psychiatrist
31%	Shelter
12%	Marriage counselor
13%	Doctor
19%	Parent/supportive relative
8%	Don't know

(Questions 71-78)
How common are the following situations when
a man and a woman have a fight—do they occur often,
sometimes, or rarely?

71. He says nasty things to hurt her.

48%	Often
33%	Sometimes
11%	Rarely
8%	Don't know

72. She says nasty things to hurt him.

40%	Often
34%	Sometimes
13%	Rarely
9%	Don't know

73. He grabs her and shoves her.

24%	Often
33%	Sometimes
30%	Rarely
13%	Don't know

74. She grabs and shoves him.

11%	Often
29%	Sometimes
48%	Rarely
12%	Don't know

75. He throws something at her.

    13%   Often
    26%   Sometimes
    49%   Rarely
    13%   Don't know

76. She throws something at him.

    26%   Often
    29%   Sometimes
    34%   Rarely
    11%   Don't know

77. He beats her up badly.

    19%   Often
    25%   Sometimes
    43%   Rarely
    13%   Don't know

78. She beats him up badly.

     5%   Often
    11%   Sometimes
    72%   Rarely
    13%   Don't know

Now I am going to read you some situations. Please tell me at what point a fight between a husband and wife becomes someone else's business.

79. When he screams at her and says abusive things.

    16%   Yes   [Ask Questions 80 and 81]
    77%   No   [Go to Questions 82]
     7%   Don't know   [Go to Questions 82]

80. [If yes] Should he be arrested?
    [Of 16% who said yes]

    12%   Yes
    73%   No
     6%   Up to wife
     9%   Don't know

81. Should she leave him?
    [Of 16% who said yes]
    39%   Yes
    34%   No
    27%   Don't know

82. When he threatens to hurt her.
    66%   Yes   [Ask Questions 83 and 84]
    28%   No   [Go to Question 85]
     6%   Don't know [Go to Question 85]

83. [If yes] Should he be arrested?
    [Of 66% who said yes]
    32%   Yes
    42%   No
    12%   Up to wife
    14%   Don't know

84. Should she leave him?
    [Of 66% who said yes]
    51%   Yes
    22%   No
    27%   Don't know

85. When he grabs her and shoves her.
    71%   Yes   [Ask Questions 86 and 87]
    23%   No   [Go to Question 88]
     6%   Don't know [Go to Question 88]

86. [If yes] Should he be arrested?
    [Of 71% who said yes]
    46%   Yes
    30%   No
    12%   Up to wife
    11%   Don't know

87. Should she leave him?
    [Of 71% who said yes]
    57%   Yes
    18%   No
    25%   Don't know

88. When he slaps her hard across the face.

86%	Yes	[Ask Questions 89 and 90]
10%	No	[Go to Question 91]
4%	Don't know	[Go to Question 91]

89. [If yes] Should he be arrested?
    [Of 86% who said yes]

61%	Yes
17%	No
11%	Up to wife
10%	Don't know

90. Should she leave him?
    [Of 86% who said yes]

66%	Yes
13%	No
22%	Don't know

91. When he punches her in the face or other parts of her body?

94%	Yes	[Ask Questions 92 and 93]
4%	No	[Go to Question 94]
2%	Don't know	[Go to Question 94]

92. [If yes] Should he be arrested?
    [Of 94% who said yes]

85%	Yes
3%	No
8%	Up to wife
4%	Don't know

93. Should she leave him?
    [Of 94% who said yes]

80%	Yes
5%	No
15%	Don't know

(Questions 94-100)
Here are some statements that people have
made about family violence. Please tell me if
you strongly agree, agree, disagree, or
disagree strongly with each statement:

94. Beating up on women is often learned in the home. Some people learn to be violent because when they were young, they were beaten or witnessed violence in their home.

51%	Strongly agree
37%	Agree
6%	Disagree
3%	Disagree strongly
2%	Don't know

95. Men who beat women do it to humiliate and bully them.

27%	Strongly agree
45%	Agree
19%	Disagree
3%	Disagree strongly
5%	Don't know

96. People may say it is wrong to hit women, but the constant pictures of women getting beaten, raped, or terrorized on television and in movies say that this violence is acceptable.

22%	Strongly agree
26%	Agree
29%	Disagree
21%	Disagree strongly
3%	Don't know

97. As long as women are economically dependent on men, they will be potential victims of violence.

23%	Strongly agree
38%	Agree
25%	Disagree
10%	Disagree strongly
3%	Don't know

98. As long as women are emotionally dependent on men, they will be potential victims of violence.

26%	Strongly agree
45%	Agree
19%	Disagree
6%	Disagree strongly
3%	Don't know

99. Violence against women is more than a physical assault. It is an attack on a woman's dignity and freedom.

49%	Strongly agree
43%	Agree
6%	Disagree
1%	Disagree strongly
2%	Don't know

100. Men who beat up their wives are using physical force to get their way.

36%	Strongly agree
50%	Agree
10%	Disagree
2%	Disagree strongly
2%	Don't know

101. Which of the following comes closest to your view of why a man would beat a women?

20%	He got drunk and lost control/didn't mean to do it
23%	He was beaten when he was young/saw his mother beaten
9%	Acting out cultural image/thinks men need to be aggressive and women submissive
5%	Trying to rob her of her hope, confidence, and self-esteem
34%	He wants to control her/thinks this will scare her into obeying him
9%	Don't know

102. Can anything be done to reduce the amount of violence against women?

81%	Yes	[Ask Question 103]
6%	No	[Go to Question 104]
13%	Don't know	[Go to Question 104]

103. [If yes] What can be done to reduce violence? [Do not read] [Of 81% who said yes]

6%	More arrests
27%	More counseling
18%	Teach kids in school
7%	Change society
5%	Reduce violence in the media/change TV
1%	Less drinking

8%	Women become less emotionally dependent and economically dependent on men
1%	Give women more pay
4%	More respect
1%	More families where the mother should stay home and not have to work
12%	Stronger laws
2%	More church
9%	Don't know

(Questions 104-109)
Suppose I wanted to get people to become more
involved in helping reduce violence against women.
Let me read you some statistics (actual facts).
Please tell me if you think hearing this would
get people to want to work on reducing violence against women.

104. More women are injured or killed by being beaten than in car accidents, muggings, and rapes combined. Do you believe that this statement is true?

55%	Yes
29%	No
16%	Don't know

105. If it were true, would this get people to pay more attention to the issues of women being beaten?

81%	Yes
13%	No
6%	Don't know

106. Every 15 seconds a woman is beaten by her husband or boyfriend. Do you believe this statement is true?

72%	Yes
15%	No
13%	Don't know

107. If it were true, would this get people to pay more attention to the issue of women being beaten?

76%	Yes
17%	No
7%	Don't know

108. Juvenile delinquents are four times more likely to come from homes in which their fathers beat their mothers. Do you believe this statement is true?

79%   Yes
14%   No
 7%   Don't know

109. If it were true, would this get people to pay more attention to the issue of women being beaten?

68%   Yes
22%   No
 9%   Don't know

Now I am going to read you some scripts of television ads. Please visualize each ad in your mind and tell me if you think it would be effective.

Sample A

110. A frightened young girl and boy are staring at you wide-eyed and terrified by having just seen their father beat their mother. A man's voice is heard over their frozen faces saying, "Today these children saw something they will never forget. Family violence hurts everyone. Break the chain now." Would you find this ad effective?

92%   Yes
 5%   No
 4%   Don't know

111. What about the slogan—"Break the chain now"—do you think that is effective?

74%   Yes
18%   No
 8%   Don't know

112. A picture of a dead woman in a body bag fills your television screen. A man's voice says, "Some women will never talk to anyone about being abused. It's up to us." Would you find this ad effective?

76%   Yes
19%   No
 5%   Don't know

113. What about the slogan—"It's up to us"—do you think that is effective?

    70%   Yes
    24%   No
     6%   Don't know

114. Which one of these two advertisements do you think would be more effective—the one with the children or the one with the woman?

    60%   Children
    24%   Woman
    13%   Both
     2%   Neither
     1%   Don't know

Sample B

110. A badly bruised woman is crying behind a closed bathroom door. Her husband is banging on the other side of the door, apologizing for hitting her and promising never to do it again. The banging gets harder and he gets angrier because she won't open the door. A man's voice is heard over a still picture of her frozen, tear-stained face—"When there is family violence, it is part of an endless chain. A man who beats a woman says his father beat his mother. Then he beats his girlfriend, wife, and next wife. His children learn from him, and their children learn from them. It's endless. We must end the pain. Break the chain now." Would this ad be effective?

    85%   Yes
     9%   No
     5%   Don't know

111. How about the slogan—"We must end the pain. Break the chain now"—is that effective?

    78%   Yes
    16%   No
     5%   Don't know

112. A little girl is playing with her Ken and Barbie dolls in her bedroom. The little girl speaking through the Barbie doll tells the father (the Ken doll) she cooked spaghetti, his favorite meal for dinner. The Ken doll says, "I don't want spaghetti, I want steak." And starts hitting the Barbie doll on her face and body. The Barbie doll says, "Yes dear, right away dear, I'm sorry I made a mistake dear." The Ken doll screams, "You can't do anything

right!" A man's voice then comes on and says, "If a woman is suffering from abuse, her children are too. Break the cycle of violence." Would this ad be effective?

87%	Yes
10%	No
3%	Don't know

113. How about the slogan—"If a woman is suffering from abuse, her children are too. Break the cycle of violence."—is that effective?

87%	Yes
9%	No
3%	Don't know

114. Which of these two advertisements do you think would be more effective. The one with the little girl or the one with the battered woman?

49%	Little girl
30%	Woman
16%	Both
3%	Neither
2%	Don't know

115. What is your age?

13%	18 to 24
24%	25 to 34
24%	35 to 44
16%	45 to 54
22%	55 and over

116. What is your race?

78%	White
12%	African American
7%	Latino/Hispanic
2%	Asian
1%	Native American
1%	Other

117. What is your personal total annual income?

26%	Less than $15,000
20%	$15,000 to $25,000
17%	$25,000 to $35,000
9%	$35,000 to $45,000

5%	$45,000 to $55,000
3%	$55,000 to $75,000
1%	$75,000 to $100,000
2%	Over $100,000
17%	Refused to answer

118. What was the last level of schooling you received?

10%	Less than high school
30%	High school graduate
29%	Some college
21%	College graduate
9%	Postcollege graduate

119. What is your current marital status?

57%	Married
18%	Single, no partner
8%	Single, with partner
7%	Divorced/separated
11%	Widowed

120. How many children do you have?

15%	One
23%	Two
16%	Three
8%	Four
4%	Five
2%	Six
1%	Seven
1%	Eight
—	Nine
—	Ten
—	Eleven
—	Twelve
30%	None

121. Do you have daughters, sons, or both?
[of those who have children]

21%	Daughters
25%	Sons
54%	Both

122. What is your current work status?
     Full-time   [Ask Question 123]
     Part-time   [Ask Question 123]
     Unemployed   [Go to Question 124]
     Homemaker   [Go to Question 124]
     Retired   [Go to Question 124]
     Student   [Go to Question 124]

123. [If employed] What is your occupation?
     1%   Military
     —   Disabled
     5%   Unemployed
     6%   Homemaker
     15%   Retired
     5%   Student
     31%   Managerial or professional
     14%   Clerical, sales, other white-collar
     15%   Blue-collar
     7%   Pink-collar
     1%   Agriculture

One last thing. To make sure I have your responses correct. Would you do any of the following to help reduce the amount of violence against women?

124. If you knew someone who was being beaten, would you talk to your friends, family, or clergy to try to figure out how to help this person?
     96%   Yes
     3%   No
     1%   Don't know

125. Would you tell the person to stop?
     82%   Yes
     10%   No
     7%   Don't know

126. Would you call the police if you saw a man beating his wife or girlfriend?
     91%   Yes
     4%   No
     5%   Don't know

127. Would you support legislation to increase funding for battered women's programs?

88%	Yes
7%	No
5%	Don't know

128. Would you give money to an organization working on this issue?

71%	Yes
18%	No
11%	Don't know

129. Would you volunteer some time and work in a program for battered women?

54%	Yes
36%	No
10%	Don't know

130. Code sex: [Do not ask]

| 50% | Female |
| 50% | Male |

131. Sample code:

| 50% | Sample A |
| 50% | Sample B |

Region code:

22%	Northeast
30%	South
28%	Midwest
5%	Mountain
15%	Pacific

Interviewer sex:

| 70% | Female |
| 30% | Male |

NOTES

1. The instruction "do not read" indicates that what follows are categories of replies to an open-ended question, not choices offered to the subjects.

2. The dash means that less than .5% responded in this way.

Appendix C
Lieberman Research, Inc., Polls

Background and Objectives

The Advertising Council, in conjunction with the Family Violence Prevention Fund, launched a national campaign starting the end of July 1994 for the prevention of domestic violence. In February 1996, a second stage of the campaign was launched, which introduced several new advertisements for the prevention of domestic violence.

The purpose of these advertising campaigns is to increase public awareness of the prevalence of domestic violence and to motivate individuals to take action to reduce and prevent domestic violence.

The purpose of the Lieberman survey is to monitor the effectiveness of the Family Violence Prevention Fund's campaign. To do this, a tracking study is being conducted that consists of a *benchmark, pre-advertising* wave or survey for the first set of advertisements and several *post-advertising introduction* waves or surveys. This wave will serve as a post-advertising wave for the original campaign and a benchmark wave for the new campaign.

The purpose of the study is to track over time:

1. Awareness of the advertising campaign
2. The public's awareness and acknowledgment that domestic violence is a serious problem
3. The public's attitudes toward domestic violence, specifically their level of intolerance
4. The public's willingness to take action against domestic violence.

I. Base Wave—July 1994

Methodology for Base Wave

This benchmark wave consists of 735 computer-assisted telephone interviews (CATIs) with women and men 18 to 65 years of age.

Respondents were screened from a random digit dial (RDD) sample and interviews were divided evenly by gender (half women, half men).

The study was conducted among residents in the 81 markets monitored for Advertising Council public service broadcast advertising.

The survey consisted of two samples—a *random sample* of about 600 interviews and an *augment sample* of about 135 interviews in California. Because the random sample yielded about 75 California interviews, this means that there were about 210 California interviews, in total, in the survey.

The interviews were divided equally among high, medium, and low media-delivery markets, based on a pre-analysis of Advertising Council media delivery in each market. Interviewing was divided in this fashion to ensure that there were enough interviews from high media-delivery markets in the sample for analytic purposes.

The interviews from high, medium, and low media-delivery markets, as well as those from California, were weighted in relation to their actual incidence in the population. In addition, the educational level of respondents was weighted to census information.

The interviewing was conducted between July 18 and 31, 1994.

For the total sample, the results have a 4% margin of error (when the percentages are at or about the 50% level).

A Note on the O. J. Simpson Trial

The murders of Nicole Brown Simpson and Ronald Goldman and the subsequent arrest of O. J. Simpson took place just prior to this survey. These events as well as the media coverage and analysis of them obviously had an influence on the attitudes and opinions about domestic violence expressed in this survey. Readers are reminded to keep these events in mind when analyzing survey results.

Overview of Base Wave Findings

Importance of Domestic Violence as a Social Issue

In this survey, most respondents said they believe that domestic violence is an important social issue. About 35% reported that it is an *extremely* important issue to them personally, whereas almost 80% reported that it is an *extremely* or *very* important issue.

Compared with other social issues, domestic violence is seen to be as important as street crime and children living in poverty and more important than the environment, teenage alcoholism, and teenage pregnancy.

Prevalence of Domestic Violence

Domestic violence occurs frequently in our society. Almost 30% of July 1994 respondents reported that they know a woman who is currently a victim of physical abuse.

To obtain further input into how widespread Americans think domestic violence is, survey respondents were asked to estimate what percentage of men have physically abused their wives or girlfriends at least once.

Respondents estimated that 49% of men, on average, had physically abused their wives or girlfriends at one time or another. Both women and men were in agreement with this 49% estimate.

When Does a Domestic Dispute Become a Public Affair?

When does a domestic dispute become a public—as opposed to a private—matter? Most respondents said they believe that disputes between couples that involve *physical violence* require other people to get involved. Disputes between couples that involve *verbal violence* were seen to be a private affair between the couple.

- 80% to 90% of respondents believe it is a *private affair* between a couple when a husband insults his wife or shouts curses at his wife and pounds his fist on the table.

- In contrast, 80% believe that *outside intervention* is required if a man hits his wife—even if she is not injured—and virtually everyone believes outside intervention is required if a man physically abuses his wife and causes injuries that require medical attention.

Actions Taken to Reduce Domestic Violence

About 18% of respondents in July 1994 said they did something in the previous year to help reduce domestic violence, such as talk to an abused woman, talk to an abusive man, donate money, or do volunteer work.

This was much lower than the number of people who did something in the previous year to help the environment (56%) or to aid children living in poverty

(43%). However, it was about the same as the number who did something about street crime (18%), teenage alcoholism (17%), and teenage pregnancy (14%).

Intent to Do Something in the Next Year

About 40% of respondents reported that they would like to do something to help reduce domestic violence in the coming year.

Two of the segments with the greatest inclination to do something were abused women and people who know someone who is abused.

Other segments with an above-average propensity to take some action to help reduce domestic abuse include *women, lower- and middle-income individuals* (household income less than $40,000), and *communities of color.*

Actions Would Take If Neighbor Was Abusing Wife

What would Americans do if a neighbor was physically abusing his wife or girlfriend? Sadly, our July 1994 respondents believe that about half of their fellow citizens would do nothing if the man next door was physically abusing his wife or girlfriend.

To the extent that some action would be taken, the most likely response would be to call the police or talk to the abused woman. Less likely responses include consulting with neighbors to decide what to do, getting involved in community action programs, and talking to the man who is abusive.

Barriers to Intervention

There are several *barriers* that must be overcome if more Americans are to get involved in reducing domestic violence.

One major barrier to doing something about domestic violence is concern about *personal safety.* About 85% of respondents in July 1994 reported that they would be concerned about their own safety if they tried to help in a specific situation of domestic violence.

Another major barrier is *lack of knowledge* about what to do. Almost two thirds of respondents reported that they don't really know what they can do to help reduce domestic violence in their community, and 70% admitted that most people would not think of joining a community action group as a way of reducing domestic violence.

In addition, there are several secondary or minor barriers to taking action against domestic violence, such as believing the police won't do anything if you call them (29%) and thinking that what happens in someone else's home is his or her own business (22%).

Rationalizations for Domestic Violence

Even though most respondents in July 1994 felt that domestic violence is an important social issue, 40% to 50% of all respondents—and an even greater proportion of men—held opinions about domestic violence that can be construed as rationalizing or justifying it.

Specifically, 47% of July 1994 respondents agreed (and 19% agreed strongly) that "men sometimes physically abuse women because they are stressed out or drunk; it's not that they mean to hurt them." And 42% agreed (and 10% agreed strongly) that "some wives provoke their husbands into physically abusing them."

Appropriate Response to Domestic Violence

What should the police do if a person is physically abusing his wife or girlfriend? Two thirds of respondents believe the police should arrest the man, whereas one third believe the police should talk to the man in his home.

Counseling or education is believed to be the most appropriate punishment for abusers by 6 out of 10 respondents. About 25% believe incarceration is most appropriate, whereas 10% support other responses (community service, fines, letting him work it out with his family or by himself).

Attitudes Toward Domestic Violence: Women Versus Men

There was a big gender gap on attitudes toward domestic violence in the July 1994 Lieberman survey. Women took the problem more seriously than men—although both groups agreed that it is an important issue—and women were less likely than men to accept rationalizations for it.

Some of the key differences between women and men include:

- Women were *more* likely than men to believe that domestic violence is an extremely important social issue (42% vs. 27%).
- Women overwhelmingly believe that abusers should be arrested (77% arrest, 21% talk to him), whereas men were more equally divided in their opinion as to the appropriate response (54% arrest, 48% talk to him).
- Women were less likely than men to accept various rationalizations of domestic violence.
- Men were more likely than women to believe that an argument in another couple's home is "none of my business" (29% vs. 15%).
- Men were more likely to believe that the problem of domestic violence has been exaggerated by the media (39% vs. 22%).

Media Stories on Domestic Violence

The O. J. Simpson case was being covered in the media at the time this survey was conducted in July 1994. Survey respondents—as well as other Americans— were very aware of these news stories. Almost 80% reported having seen media stories on domestic violence *very often* or *fairly often* in the previous 3 months.

Respondents reported that these media stories made them more likely to take some action to help reduce domestic violence (47% more likely vs. 6% less likely vs. 47% no effect).

Domestic Violence Advertising

Even though the Family Violence Prevention Fund advertising campaign on domestic violence did not begin until after the July 1994 survey was completed, reported awareness of domestic violence advertising was high. Unaided awareness of domestic violence advertising was 22%, whereas total awareness of domestic violence advertising was 64%.

The high reported awareness levels for advertising about domestic violence may be the result of confusion in memory between media stories about domestic violence—which had been in the news extensively—and advertising about domestic violence.

There is some evidence in the survey to support this theory. In July 1994, respondents who saw media stories about domestic violence *very often* in the previous 3 months were more likely than those who saw media stories *less than very often* to report awareness of domestic violence advertising.

II. Post-Wave I—November 1994-February 1995

Methodology for Post-Wave I

This wave of interviewing was conducted 4 to 7 months after the campaign first aired. It consisted of 982 CATIs divided evenly across 4 months (about 243 interviews in each month, November 1994 to February 1995). The sample was made up of women and men 18 to 65 years of age. Respondents were screened from an RDD sample and interviews were divided evenly by gender (half women, half men).

The study was conducted among residents in the 81 markets monitored for Advertising Council public service broadcast advertising.

The survey consisted of two samples—a *random sample* of about 800 interviews and an *augment sample* of about 175 interviews in California.

Because the random sample yielded about 100 California interviews, there were about 275 California interviews, in total, in the survey.

The interviews were divided equally between high, medium, and low media-delivery markets, based on a pre-analysis of Advertising Council media delivery in each market. Interviewing was divided in this fashion to ensure that there were enough interviews from high media-delivery markets in the sample for analytic purposes.

The interviews from high, medium, and low media-delivery markets, as well as those from California, were weighted in relation to their actual incidence in the population. In addition, the educational level of respondents was weighted to census information.

The interviewing was conducted from November 1994 through February 1995. For the total sample, the results have a 3% margin of error (when the percentages are at or about the 50% level).

Overview of Post-Wave I Findings

Background: Media Stories on Domestic Violence

Respondents continued to be very aware of coverage of the O. J. Simpson trial. Over 70% reported that they had seen media stories on domestic violence *very* or *fairly* often in the previous 3 months, and fully 45% had seen media stories *very* often.

Respondents in post-wave I reported that these media stories had made them more likely to take some action to help reduce domestic violence (50% more likely, vs. 5% less likely, vs. 45% no effect).

Domestic Violence Advertising

Despite the O. J. Simpson trial, the domestic violence advertising campaign was getting to the public and being remembered.

- Aided recall of the three domestic violence advertisements increased significantly between the July 1994 base wave and January-February 1995.
- Awareness of "Hear violent fight, neighbors decide how to react" increased from 22% to 35%; awareness of "42% of all murdered women are killed by the same man" increased from 30% to 37%; and awareness of "If the noise next door were music, you'd do something" increased from 25% to 29%.

- Awareness of the campaign's lead TV advertisement—"Hear violent fight, neighbors decide how to react"—showed the strongest gains in awareness.
- All three advertisements from the domestic violence campaign were recalled at higher levels than a fictitious ad about domestic violence. From 29% to 37% of respondents recalled each of the advertisements from the domestic violence campaign, compared with only 23% who recalled the fictitious ad.

Although aided recall of the three specific advertisements from the domestic violence campaign increased compared with that of the July 1994 campaign, standard tracking study measures of unaided and total advertising awareness remained basically unchanged during this time period.

Importance of Domestic Violence as a Social Issue

As was the case in July 1994, most respondents to post-wave I believe that domestic violence is an important social issue. About 36% reported that it is an *extremely* important social issue, whereas fully 80% reported that it is an *extremely* or *very* important social issue.

Compared with other social issues, domestic violence was seen to be more important than teenage alcoholism and teenage pregnancy, about as important as children living in poverty and the environment, but less important than street crime.

Incidence of Domestic Violence

Domestic violence occurs frequently in our society. About 40% of women respondents reported that they had been physically abused or threatened with physical abuse at one time or another; about 30% had been victims of physical abuse, and about 10% had been threatened with physical abuse (but never actually abused).

To obtain another perspective on the prevalence of domestic violence, survey respondents were asked if they know any women who are physically abused by their husbands or boyfriends.

Consistent with the previous finding, about 30% of post-wave I respondents reported that they know someone who is currently a victim of physical abuse.

Interestingly, there was an increase between July 1994 and November 1994-February 1995 in the proportion of women who reported that they had been victims of domestic violence and in the proportion of women who reported that they know someone who is being physically abused.

The causes of these increases are not entirely clear from the survey. Possibly, women felt freer to talk about domestic violence and their experiences with it. Another possibility is that women were redefining what counts as domestic violence and, as a result, saw themselves as victims.

Severity of Domestic Violence

Most women respondents who said they had been physically abused reported that they had been hurt or injured by the abuse, and close to one half reported that it occurred frequently—once a month or more often. Most physically abused women in the post-wave I survey believe that the abuse is an attempt on the part of the man to control or intimidate them with violence.

From these findings, we can extrapolate that fully 76% of women who have been physically abused, or 24% of *total* American women, have been hurt or injured by domestic violence at one time in their life.[1]

Notably, only one quarter of physically abused women in the post-wave I survey reported that it happened only once.

Percentage of Men Who Are Thought to Be Abusive

To obtain further input into how widespread Americans think domestic violence is, survey respondents were asked to estimate what percentage of men have ever physically abused their wives or girlfriends.

Respondents in post-wave I estimated that 49% of men, on average, have physically abused their wives or girlfriends at one time or another. Both men and women were in agreement with this 49% estimate.

Changes in Attitudes About Domestic Violence

Although consciousness of domestic violence as an important social issue had started at fairly high levels in July 1994, the public had grown more intolerant of it during the 7 months before post-wave I was completed, that is between July 1994 and February 1995. In post-wave I,

- Most respondents agreed that outside intervention is required if a man hits his wife—even if she is not injured (87% vs. 80% in July 1994).
- More respondents believe that outside intervention is required if a man exhibits threatening behavior by "shouting curses at his wife and pounding his fist on the table" (28% vs. 19% in July 1994).

- There had been a decline in the proportion of respondents believing that "the problem of domestic violence has been exaggerated by the media" (24% vs. 30% in July 1994).

- Fewer respondents said they believe that "since the police don't do anything anyway, it isn't very helpful to report that a man is physically abusing a woman" (18% vs. 29% in July 1994).

- Among men respondents, there had also been an increase in advocating that abusers be arrested (57% vs. 49% in July 1994).

Actions Taken to Reduce Domestic Violence

The increased intolerance of domestic violence had been translated, among women, into action to reduce it. One quarter of women respondents in post-wave I reported that they had done something in the previous year to help reduce domestic violence, compared with 19% who had done something in July 1994. There were significant increases in talking to an abused woman, and more modest increases for other actions such as talking to an abusive man, calling the police, donating money, and so on.

Although the overall level of doing something about domestic violence did *not* increase among men respondents between July 1994 and post-wave I, men in the second wave had a somewhat greater propensity to call the police when they suspect domestic violence.

Intent to Do Something in the Next Year

About 41% of respondents to post-wave I reported that they intend to do something to reduce domestic violence in the coming year.

Two of the segments with the greatest inclination to do something were *abused women* and *people who know someone who has been abused.*

Demographically, the segments with an above-average propensity to take some action to reduce domestic violence include women, lower-income individuals (less than $20,000 household income), and California residents.

Actions Would Take If Neighbor Was Abusing Wife

What would Americans do if a neighbor was physically abusing his wife or girlfriend? Sadly, respondents in post-wave I were more convinced than respondents in July 1994 that the majority of their fellow citizens would do nothing if the man next door was physically abusing his wife or girlfriend.

To the extent that some action would be taken, the most likely response would be to call the police or talk to the abused woman. Less likely responses include consulting with neighbors to decide what to do, getting involved in community action programs, and talking to the man who is abusive.

Barriers to Intervention

There are several *barriers* that must be overcome if more Americans are to get involved in reducing domestic violence.

One major barrier to doing something about domestic violence is concern about *personal safety*. About 84% of respondents in post-wave I reported that they would be concerned about their own safety if they tried to help in a specific situation of domestic violence.

Another major barrier is *lack of knowledge* about what to do. More than 60% of respondents to the post-wave I survey reported that they don't really know what they can do to help reduce domestic violence in their community, and over 70% admitted that most people would not think of joining a community action group as a way of reducing domestic violence.

In addition, there are several secondary or minor barriers to taking action against domestic violence, such as thinking that what happens in someone else's home is their own business (22%) and believing the police won't do anything if you call them (18%).

Rationalizations for Domestic Violence

Even though most respondents felt that domestic violence is an important social issue, 40% to 50% of total respondents—and an even greater proportion of men—held opinions about domestic violence that can be construed as rationalizing or justifying it.

Specifically, 46% of post-wave I respondents agreed (and 21% agreed strongly) that "men sometimes physically abuse women because they are stressed out or drunk; it's not that they mean to hurt them." And 41% agreed (14% agreed strongly) that "some wives provoke their husbands into physically abusing them."

Appropriate Response to Domestic Violence

What should the police do if a man is physically abusing his wife or girlfriend? Two thirds of respondents to the post-wave I survey said they believe the police should arrest the man, whereas 3 out of 10 believe the police should talk to the man in his home.

About 63% of respondents advocate counseling or education for domestic abusers. About 25% believe incarceration is most appropriate, whereas 10%

support other responses (community service, fines, letting him work out his problem with his family or by himself).

Attitudes About Domestic Violence: Women Versus Men

There is a big gender gap on attitudes about domestic violence. Women respondents in post-wave I took the problem more seriously than men—although both groups agreed that it is an important issue—and women were less likely than men to accept rationalizations for it.

Some of the key differences between women and men include:

- Women were more likely than men to believe that domestic violence is an important social issue (86% vs. 73%).

- Women were more likely than men to believe that abusers should be arrested (70% vs. 57%), whereas men were *more* likely to believe that the police should talk to the abuser in his home (38% vs. 22%).

- Women were *less* likely than men to accept various rationalizations for domestic violence.

- Men were more likely than women to believe that an argument in another couple's home is "none of my business" (31% vs. 21%).

- Men were more likely to believe that the problem of domestic violence has been exaggerated by the media (31% vs. 15%).

Linking the Ad Council Campaign to Changing Attitudes About Domestic Violence

The survey results suggest that the domestic violence advertising campaign contributed to the changes in attitudes and behavior seen between July 1993 and post-wave I, November 1994 to February 1995, a period of 7 months.

In markets receiving *heavy* media delivery of the domestic violence campaign, there were somewhat greater increases than in other markets in recall of domestic violence advertising and in taking action to reduce domestic violence. There was also increased advocacy of counseling/education in heavy media-delivery markets and rejection of the notion that the abusive man should work out his problem by himself.

In heavy media-delivery markets, there was also increased confusion among some of the public about what can be done about the problem. This was expressed in increased agreement with statements like "I don't really know what I can do to help reduce domestic violence," "Most people wouldn't think of joining a community action group as a way of reducing domestic violence," and "I would be hesitant to talk to an abused woman about her abuse."

The implication of these findings is that while the Advertising Council campaign motivated people to take action against domestic violence, people still do not know how to get involved. Future phases of the campaign should address this more specifically.

California

The trends in attitudes about domestic violence in California are different from those in the rest of the country. Some of the key differences in California compared with the remainder of the United States include:

- The domestic violence campaign was not as successful in California in cutting through the clutter and being remembered. Unaided awareness of domestic violence advertising decreased in California between July 1994 and November1994-February 1995, whereas recall of specific domestic violence ads remained relatively unchanged.
- Californians increased their commitment to take action against domestic violence more than people in the rest of the country. Intentions to do something about domestic violence increased in California between July 1994 and post-wave I, as did advocacy of incarceration for domestic abusers.
- In contrast to other Americans, Californians became increasingly concerned about what would happen to their own safety if they were to try to stop a specific situation of domestic violence and, as a result, they were increasingly hesitant about talking to physically abused women about their abuse.

These concerns and attitudes may indicate that the violence of the Nicole Brown Simpson and Ronald Goldman murders had a greater impact in California—the state where the incident occurred—than in the rest of the country.

III. Post-Wave II—November 1995

Methodology for Post-Wave II

This wave of interviewing was conducted 16 months after the original campaign first aired. It consists of 742 CATIs with women and men 18 to 65 years of age.

Respondents were screened from a RDD sample and interviews were divided evenly by gender.

The study was conducted among residents in the 81 markets monitored for Advertising Council public service broadcast advertising.

The survey consisted of two samples—a *random sample* of 610 interviews and an *augment sample* of 132 interviews in California. Because the random sample yielded 70 California interviews, there were 202 California interviews, in total, in the survey.

The interviews were divided equally between high, medium, and low media-delivery markets, based on a pre-analysis of Advertising Council media delivery in each market. Interviewing was divided in this fashion to ensure that there were enough interviews from high media-delivery markets in the sample for analytic purposes.

The interviews from high, medium, and low media-delivery markets, as well as those from California, were weighted in relation to their actual incidence in the population. In addition, the educational level of respondents was weighted to census information.

The interviewing was conducted from November 9 to 20, 1995.

For the total sample, the results have a 4% margin of error (when the percentages are at or about the 50% level).

Overview of Post-Wave II Findings

Background: Media Stories on Domestic Violence

Respondents to post-wave II were very aware of media stories about domestic violence. About 67% reported that they had seen media stories on domestic violence *very* or *fairly* often in the previous 3 months, whereas fully 39% had seen media stories *very* often.

Respondents continued to report that these media stories made them more likely to take some action to help reduce domestic violence (49% more likely vs. 5% less likely vs. 46% no effect).

Media Coverage of the O. J. Simpson Trial

Most respondents said they learned about domestic violence from the media coverage of the O. J. Simpson trial. Over 70% reported learning *something* about domestic violence from the media coverage, whereas almost half (48%) believe they learned *a lot* or *a fair amount*.

Respondents to the post-wave II survey said they learned several things about domestic violence from the media coverage of the O. J. Simpson trial. Most learned that

- Domestic violence is a serious problem.

- Women who are physically abused are more likely than other women to be killed by their husbands.
- Most people need to find out more about how to handle domestic violence, including public officals.

Domestic Violence Advertising

By the time of the post-wave II survey in November 1995, the domestic violence advertising campaign was reaching the public and being remembered.

- Aided recall of the three domestic violence advertisements currently on-air increased significantly between post-wave I and post-wave II.

Awareness of "Hear violent fight, neighbors decide how to react" increased from 35% to 41%; awareness of "42% of all murdered women are killed by the same man" increased from 37% to 47%; and awareness of "If the noise next door were music, you'd do something" increased from 29% to 39%.

- All three advertisements from the domestic violence campaign were recalled at higher levels than a fictitious ad about domestic violence. About 39% to 47% of respondents recalled each of the advertisements from the domestic violence campaign, compared with only 22% who claimed to recall the fictitious ad.
- Unaided and total advertising awareness also increased significantly between post-wave I and post-wave II in November 1995. Unaided awareness increased from 22% to 31%, whereas total awareness increased from 63% to 73%.

Aided Recall of New Ads

Claimed aided recall of two out of the three new ads not yet on-air in November 1995 was in line with base wave levels of recall as seen in previous tracking waves. Claimed aided recall of "While you're trying to find the right words, your friend may be trying to stay alive" is 19%; and claimed aided recall of "It's hard to confront a friend who abuses his wife, but not nearly as hard as being his wife" is 12%.

The third new advertisement, "Children have to sit by and watch, but there are things that the rest of us can do to help," elicits unusually high base-wave levels of claimed recall. This suggests that there may be media stories, advertisements, or even television movies on-air featuring children in similar situations.

Awareness of 1-800-END-ABUSE

About 32% of respondents to post-wave II claimed to recall 1-800-END-ABUSE, the direct response phone number featured in the new advertisements not yet on-air in November 1995. As this is the base wave for the new number, claimed recall is unusually high, suggesting confusion among the public between this phone number and the numerous other domestic violence numbers and hotlines.

Importance of Domestic Violence as a Social Issue

As was the case in post-wave I, most respondents to post-wave II believe that domestic violence is an important social issue. About 38% reported that it is an *extremely* important social issue, whereas fully 83% report that it is an *extremely* or *very* important social issue.

Compared with other social issues, domestic violence is seen to be more important than the environment, teenage alcoholism, and teenage pregnancy, and as important as children living in poverty and street crime.

Incidence of Domestic Violence

Domestic violence continues to occur frequently in our society. About 30% of women respondents reported that they have been physically abused by their husband or boyfriend at one time or another.

To obtain another perspective on the prevalence of domestic violence, survey respondents were asked if they know any women who are physically abused by their husbands or boyfriends.

Consistent with previous findings, more than one out of every three respondents to post-wave II reported that they know someone who is currently a victim of physical abuse.

Severity of Domestic Violence

Most women respondents who said they had been physically abused reported that they had been hurt or injured by the abuse.

We can extrapolate from these findings that fully 81% of women who have been physically abused or 24% of *total* American women reported that they have been hurt or injured by domestic violence at one time in their life.

Notably, 28% of abused women respondents reported that the abuse happened frequently, whereas 57% reported that it happened frequently or occasionally. Less than one half reported that it happened rarely.

History of Physical Abuse

Women respondents who were physically abused by a husband or boyfriend were more likely than other women to come from physically abusive backgrounds. One third reported they grew up in a household where their mother was physically abused, and about one in five victims of physical abuse were themselves abused as children or teenagers.

On a brighter side, there is a note of hope. About one third to one half of women who came from abusive households managed to avoid abuse in their adult lives, reporting that they had never been physically abused by a husband or boyfriend. However, one quarter of women who did not come from physically abusive households reported having been physically abused by a husband or boyfriend.

Perceived Extensiveness of Domestic Violence

In order to obtain further input into how widespread Americans think domestic violence is, survey respondents were asked to estimate what percentage of men have ever physically abused their wives or girlfriends at least once.

Respondents to post-wave II estimated that one half of all men, on average, have physically abused their wives or girlfriends at one time or another.

Changes in Attitudes About Domestic Violence

Although attitudes about domestic violence changed only slightly between post-wave I and post-wave II, attitudes seem to be polarizing.

More Americans in post-wave II believe that they know what they can do to help reduce domestic violence in their community. However, other Americans are moving in the opposite direction and believe it's not their business when a husband physically abuses his wife during an argument inside the couple's own home.

There were only minor changes between post-wave I and post-wave II in attitudes toward domestic violence among both women and men.

Actions Taken to Reduce Domestic Violence

Although attitudes about domestic violence changed only slightly between post-wave I and post-wave II, there was a continuing trend, beginning with the base wave in July 1994, in taking action against it.

About 24% of post-wave II respondents reported that they have done something in the past year to help reduce domestic violence. This represents an increase from 21% in post-wave I and 18% in the base wave.

The most common actions to help reduce domestic violence were to discuss how to stop it with friends/coworkers and to talk directly to an abused woman.

The two groups most likely, by far, to do something about domestic violence were abused women and people who know someone who is being abused.

Of note is that the increases in taking action against domestic violence occurred among women exclusively. Among men, there were no significant increases in taking action against domestic violence since the base wave in July 1994.

Intent to Do Something in the Next Year

About 41% of respondents to post-wave II reported that they intend to do something to reduce domestic violence in the coming year.

As before, the two segments with the greatest inclination to do something were abused women and people who know an abused woman.

Demographically, the segments with an above-average propensity to take some action to reduce domestic violence include women, city residents, and California residents.

Actions Would Take If Neighbor Was Abusing Wife

What would Americans do if a neighbor was physically abusing his wife or girlfriend? Sadly, respondents to post-wave II continued to believe that the majority of their fellow citizens would do nothing if the man next door was physically abusing his wife or girlfriend. However, this number had not increased since post-wave I, November 1994 to February 1995.

To the extent that some action would be taken, the most likely responses were calling the police or talking to the abused woman. Somewhat less likely responses include consulting with neighbors, seeking advice from local domestic violence programs, or talking to the abusive man.

Actions Might Take Against Domestic Violence

Respondents to post-wave II in November 1995 said they would be willing to take a variety of actions to help raise awareness and reduce domestic violence. The actions they would be most willing to take include honking to draw attention if a man is hitting a woman; wearing T-shirts or buttons that say "There is no excuse for domestic violence"; and putting a "There's no excuse for domestic violence" bumper sticker on their car.

The majority of the public would also be willing to take other, more committed action such as distributing information at work, asking clergy to speak on the matter, calling or writing to elected officials to ask them to do more about domestic violence, and contacting local television or radio stations to ask them to run public service announcements about domestic violence.

Possibly, some of these actions can be used to help draw people who do *not* know about specific situations of abuse into the fight against domestic violence.

Barriers to Intervention

There continue to be several *barriers* that must be overcome if more Americans are to get involved in reducing domestic violence.

One major barrier to doing something about domestic violence continues to involve concern about *personal safety*. About 84% of respondents to post-wave II reported that they would be concerned about their own safety if they tried to help in a specific situation of domestic violence.

Another major barrier to intervention involves lack of knowledge about what to do. About 82% of respondents said they would do something to help reduce domestic violence if they knew of a way to help other than by addressing a specific instance of domestic violence, and over 75% admitted that most people wouldn't think of seeking advice from a local domestic violence program about what to do to help reduce domestic violence.

Finally, there are several secondary barriers to taking action to reduce domestic violence. Almost 40% of respondents to post-wave II said they wouldn't know what to say to an abused woman or an abusive man. More than 25% believe it is none of their business when a man abuses his wife during an argument in their own home, and about 20% believe the police won't do anything if they report a situation of domestic violence.

Rationalizations for Domestic Violence

Even though most believe that domestic violence is an important social issue, 38% to 46% of respondents—and an even greater proportion of men—held opinions about domestic violence that can be construed as rationalizing or justifying it.

Specifically, 46% of respondents to post-wave II agreed that "men sometimes physically abuse women because they are stressed out or drunk; it's not that they mean to hurt them."

And, 38% agreed that "some wives provoke their husbands into physically abusing them."

Appropriate Response to Domestic Violence

What should the police do if a man is physically abusing his wife or girlfriend? About two thirds of respondents to post-wave II believe the police should arrest the man, whereas about 3 out of 10 believe the police should talk to the man in his home.

Most respondents, 63%, continue to advocate counseling or education for domestic abusers. About 27% believe incarceration is most appropriate, whereas 10% support other responses (community service, fines, letting him work out his problem with his family or by himself).

Attitudes About Domestic Violence:
Women Versus Men

There is a big gender gap on attitudes about domestic violence, as measured by post-wave II in November 1995. Women took the problem more seriously than men—and were less likely than men to accept rationalizations for it.

Some of the key differences between women and men include:

- Women continued to be more likely than men to say that domestic violence is an *extremely important* problem.
- Women continued to be less likely than men to accept various rationalizations for domestic violence.
- Women were more likely than men to report that they would do something to help reduce domestic violence if they knew of a way to help other than by addressing a specific instance of it.
- Women were more likely than men to advocate arresting physically abusive men, whereas men were more likely than women to believe that the police should talk to the man in this home.
- Men were *more* likely than women to believe that the problem of domestic violence is exaggerated by the media.

Linking the Ad Council Campaign to
Changing Attitudes About Domestic Violence

The survey results suggest that the domestic violence advertising campaign has contributed to changes in attitudes and behavior seen.

- Those aware of the domestic violence campaign were more likely than those not aware of the campaign to have enlightened attitudes about domestic violence and to have taken action to help reduce domestic violence in the previous year. In general, the behavioral and attitudinal differences between those aware of the campaign and those not aware of the campaign were more obvious in the November 1995 wave than they were in the July 1994 base wave.

- There were greater gains between July 1994 and November 1995 in heavy media-delivery markets than in moderate/light markets on tracking study measures such as awareness of domestic violence advertising, taking action to reduce domestic violence, the perceived importance of domestic violence as a social issue, and believing that physical abusers should be arrested and incarcerated.

These findings suggest that the domestic violence advertising campaign influenced the attitudinal and behaviorial changes seen in this study over the past 9 months.

California

The trends in attitudes in California about domestic violence are different from attitudes in the rest of the country. Some of the key differences in California compared with the remainder of the United States include:

- Californian respondents in post-wave II were more likely to have learned something about domestic violence from the media coverage of the O. J. Simpson trial than were other respondents.
- The perceived importance of domestic violence as a social issue has increased for Californian respondents since post-wave I, while remaining unchanged in the rest of the country.
- In contrast to other Americans, Californians have become less concerned about their own safety if they try to stop a specific situation of domestic violence and less likely to rationalize an occurrence of domestic violence. Fewer Californian respondents in post-wave II agreed that some wives provoke their husbands into physically abusing them.

Note

1. Women who said they had *ever* been physically abused were asked the question, "Were you *ever* hurt or injured when you were physically abused by a husband or boyfriend?" This question was added to this wave of the study. It was not asked in the July 1994 wave.

References

Advertising Research Foundation. (1991, April). *Inspiring action and saving lives: A study conducted by the Advertising Research Foundation for The Advertising Council*. New York: Author.

Agtuca, J. (1994). *A community secret, for the Filipina in an abusive relationship*. Seattle: Seal Press.

Asbury, J. (1987). African American women in violent relationships: An exploration of cultural differences. In R. H. Hampton (Ed.), *Violence in the Black family: Correlates and consequences* (pp. 89-105). Lexington, MA: Lexington Books.

Asbury, J. (1993). Violence in families of color in the United States. In R. L. Hampton, R. P. Gullott, G. R. Adams, E. Potter, II, & R. P. Weissberg (Eds.), *Family violence: Prevention and treatment* (pp. 159-175). Newbury Park, CA: Sage.

ASI Market Research, Inc. (1994, June). *Recall Plus Test*. New York: The Advertising Council and the Family Violence Prevention Fund.

Bachman, R. (1994). *Violence against women: A national crime victimization survey report*. Washington, DC: U.S. Department of Justice.

Bachman, R., & Coker, A. (1995). Police involvement in domestic violence: The interactive effects of victim injury, offender's history of violence and race. *Violence and Victims, 10*(2) 91-106.

Bachman, R., & Saltzman, L. E. (1995). *Violence against women: Estimates from the redesigned survey*. Washington, DC: U.S. Department of Justice.

Bell, C. C. (1987). Preventive strategies for dealing with violence among blacks. *Community Mental Health Journal, 23*(3), 217-228.

Cafferty, P. S. J., & Chestang, L. (1976). *The diverse society: Implications for social policy*. Washington, DC: National Association of Social Workers.

Campbell, D. W., Campbell, J. C., King, C., Parker, B., & Ryan, J. (1994). The reliability and factor structure of the Index of Spouse Abuse with African American women. *Violence and Victims, 9*(3), 259-274.

Campbell, J. C. (1991, May 17-19). *Woman abuse and woman status: Wifebeating in the era of the French Revolution*. Paper presented at the Nursing Network on Violence Against Women, Fourth National Conference on Violence Against Women.

167

Campbell, J. C., & Humphreys, J. C. (1993). *Nursing care of survivors of family violence.* Newbury Park, CA: Sage.

Campbell, J. C., Miller, P., Cardwell, M. M., & Belknap, R. A. (1994). Relationship status of battered women over time. *Journal of Family Violence, 9,* 99-111.

Campbell, J. C., Pugh, L. C., Campbell, D. W., & Visscher, M. (1995). The influence of abuse on unintended pregnancy. *Women's Health Institute, 5*(4), 214-223.

Carmody, D. C., & Williams, K. R. (1987). Wife assault and perceptions of sanctions. *Violence and Victims, 2,* 25-38.

Cazenave, N., & Strauss, M. (1979). Race, class, and network embeddedness and family violence. *Journal of Comparative Family Studies, 10,* 281-300.

Coker, A. (1992). *Effect of injury on police involvement in intimate violence.* Paper presented at the 44th Annual American Society of Criminology Meeting, New Orleans, LA.

Counts, D., Brown, J., & Campbell, J. (1992). *Sanctions and sanctuary: Cultural analysis of the beating of wives.* Boulder, CO: Westview.

Court TV. (1995, February 3). Comment made by Robert Honecker, Jr., 2nd Assistant Prosecutor of Monmouth County.

Dennis, R. E., Key, L. J., Kirk, A. L., & Smith, A. (1995). Addressing domestic violence in the African American community. *Journal of Health Care for the Poor and Underserved, 6*(2), 284-293.

Desjarlais, R., Eisenberg, L., Good, B., & Kleiman, A. (1995). *World mental health: Problems and priorities in low-income countries.* New York: Oxford University Press.

Dibble, U., & Straus, M. (1980). Some social structure determinants of inconsistency between attitudes and behavior: The case of family violence. *Journal of Marriage and the Family, 42,* 73-79.

Dobash, R. E., & Dobash, R. P. (1979). *Violence against wives.* New York: Free Press.

Dobash, R. E., & Dobash, R. P. (1992). *Women, violence and social change.* New York: Routledge.

Dutton, D. (1988). Profiling of wife assaulters: Preliminary evidence for a trimodal analysis. *Violence and Victims, 3*(1), 5-29.

Edleson, J., & Brygger, M. T. (1986). Gender differences in reports of battering incidents. *Family Relations, 35,* 377-382.

Fagan, J., & Browne, A. (1994). Violence between spouses and intimates: Physical aggression between women and men in intimate relationships. In A. Reiss & J. Roth (Eds.), *Understanding and preventing violence* (Vol. 3). Washington, DC: National Academy Press.

Gelles, R. J., & Straus, M. A. (1988). *Intimate violence: The causes and consequences of abuse in the American family.* New York: Simon & Schuster.

Gordon, L. (1988). *Heroes of their own lives: The politics and history of family violence.* New York: Viking Penguin.

Greenblat, C. (1985). "Don't hit your wife . . . unless . . .": Preliminary findings on normative support for the use of physical force by husbands. *Victimology, 10,* 221-241.

Hampton, R. L., & Coner-Edwards, A. F. W. (1993). Physician and sexual violence in marriage. In R. L. Hampton, T. P. Gulotta, G. R. Adams, E. Potter, II, & R. P. Weissberg (Eds.), *Family violence: Prevention and treatment* (pp. 113-141). Newbury Park, CA: Sage.

Hampton, R. L., & Gelles, R. J. (1993). Violence toward Black women in a nationally representative sample of Black American families. In R. L. Hampton, T. P. Gullotta, G. R. Adams, E. Potter, II, & R. P. Weissberg (Eds.), *Family violence: Prevention and treatment* (pp. 113-139). Thousand Oaks, CA: Sage.

Hampton, R. L., Gelles, R. J., & Harrop, J. (1989). Is violence in black families increasing? A comparison of 1975 and 1985 national survey rates. In R. L. Hampton (Ed.), *Black family violence: Current research and theory* (pp. 3-18). Lexington, MA: Lexington Books.

Harris, L. (1993). *The first comprehensive national health survey of American women.* New York: The Commonwealth Fund.

Heise, L., Pitanguy, J., & Germain, A. (1994). *Violence against women: The hidden health burden.* Washington, DC: The World Bank.

Hotaling, G. T., & Sugarman, D. B. (1986). A risk marker analysis of assaulted wives. *Journal of Family Violence, 5,* 1-14.

Hutchison, I., Hirschel, J., & Pesackis, C. (1994). Family violence and police utilization. *Violence and Victims, 9*(4), 299-313.

Johnson, H., & Sacco, V. (1995). Statistics Canada's national survey. *Canadian Journal of Criminology, 37*(3), 281-304.

Jouriles, E. K., & O'Leary, D. (1985). Intra-spousal reliability of reports of marital violence. *Journal of Consulting & Clinical Psychology, 3,* 419-421.

Kalichman, S. C., Kelly, J. A., Hunter, T. L., Murphy, D. A., & Tyler, R. (1993). Culturally tailored HIV-AIDS risk-reduction messages targeted to African American urban women: Impact on risk sensitization and risk reduction. *Journal of Consulting and Clinical Psychology, 61*(2), 291-295.

Kanagawa Women's Council. (1995). *For the elimination of violence against women.* Kanagawa, Japan: Kanagawa Prefecture.

Kelly, J. A., St. Lawrence, J. S., Stevenson, L. Y., Hauth, A. C., Kalichman, S. C., Diazy, E., Brasield, J. L., Koob, J. J., & Morgan, M. G. (1992). Community AIDS/HIV risk reduction: The effects of endorsements by popular people in three cities. *American Journal of Public Health, 82*(11), 1483-1489.

Kizer, K., & Honig, B. (1990). *Toward a tobacco-free California: A status report to the California Legislature on the first 15 months of California's tobacco control program.* Sacramento, CA: Department of Health Services.

Landenburger, K. (1989). A process of entrapment in and recovery from an abusive relationship. *Issues in Mental Health Nursing, 10,* 209-227.

Levinson, D. (1989). *Family violence in cross-cultural perspective.* Newbury Park, CA: Sage.

Liz Claiborne, Inc. (1994, August). *Addressing domestic violence: A corporate response* (poll conducted by Roper Starch). New York: Author.

Lockhart, L. (1985). Methodological issues in comparative racial analysis: The case of wife abuse. *Research and Abstracts, 13,* 35-41.

Lockhart, L. (1991). Spousal violence: A cross-racial perspective. In R. L. Hampton (Ed.), *Black family violence: Current research and theory* (pp. 85-102). Lexington, MA: Lexington Books.

Lockhart, L., & White, B. (1989). Understanding marital violence in the black community. *Journal of Interpersonal Violence, 4*(4), 3-4.

Lystad, M. (1986). *Violence in the home: Interdisciplinary perspectives.* New York: Brunner/Mazel.

Marin Abused Women's Services. (1993). *Man to man: A public opinion survey of men's knowledge, attitudes, beliefs, and behaviors concerning domestic violence.* San Rafael, CA: Author.

Marsella, A. J. Friedman, M. J., Gerrity, E. T., & Scurfield, R. M. (1996). Ethnocultural aspects of posttraumatic stress disorder. Washington, DC: American Psychological Association.

Martin, D. (1976). *Battered wives.* San Francisco: Glide.

Mathabane, M. (1994). *African women: Three generations.* New York: HarperCollins.

May, M. (1978). Violence in the family: An historical perspective. In D. Martin (Ed.), *Violence in the family* (pp. 135-163). Chichester, UK: John Wiley.

Miller, S. L. (1989). Unintended side effects of pro-arrest policies and their race and class implications for battered women: A cautionary note. *Criminal Justice Policy Review, 3,* 299-317.

Molina, C. W., Zambrana, & Aguirre-Molina, M. (1994). The influence of culture, class, and environment on health care. In C.W. Molina & M. Aguirre-Molina (Eds.), *Latino health in the U.S: A growing challenge.* Baltimore, MD: Victor Graphics.

Pence, E., & Shepard, M. (1988). Integrating feminist theory and practice: The challenge of the battered woman's movement. In K. Yllo & M. Bograd (Eds.), *Feminist perspectives on wife abuse* (pp. 282-298). Newbury Park, CA: Sage.

Peterson-Lewis, S., Turner, C., & Adams, A. (1986). Attributional processes in repeatedly abused women. In G. W. Russell (Ed.), *Violence in intimate relationships* (pp. 107-130). New York: PMA.

PR Solutions. (1995, March). Media audit. Washington, DC: Family Violence Prevention Fund.

Rosenberg, M., Stark, E., & Zahn, M. (1986). Interpersonal violence: Homicide and spouse abuse. In J. Last (Ed.), *Public health and preventive medicine* (12th ed., pp. 1399-1426). Norwalk, CT: Appleton Century Crofts.

Sampson, R. (1987). Urban black violence: The effect of male joblessness and family disruption. *American Journal of Sociology, 93*(2), 348-382.

San Francisco Domestic Violence Consortium. (1995, March). *Domestic violence in San Francisco: A call for public safety.* San Francisco, CA: Author.

Saunders, D. (1986). When battered women use violence: Husband abuse or self defense? *Violence and Victims, 1,* 47-60.

Schechter, S. (1982). *Women and male violence: The visions and struggles of the battered women's movement.* Boston: South End Press.

Sherman, L. W. (1992). *Policing domestic violence: Experiments and dilemmas.* New York: Free Press.

Snell, J., Rosenwald, R., & Robey, A. (1964). The wifebeater's wife. *Archives of General Psychiatry, 11,* 107-112.

Sorenson, S. B. (1996). *Violence against women: Examining ethnic differences and commonalities.* Thousand Oaks, CA: Sage.

Stark, R., & McEvoy, J. (1970). Middle-class violence. *Psychology Today, 4,* 52-56, 110-112.

Straus, M., & Gelles, R. (1986). Societal change and change in family violence from 1975-1985 as revealed by two national studies. *Journal of Marriage and the Family, 48,* 465-479.

Straus, M. A., & Gelles, R. J. (Eds.). (1990). *Physical violence in American families: Risk factors and adaptations to violence in 8,145 families.* New Brunswick: Transaction.

Straus, M. A., Gelles, R. J., & Steinmetz, S. K. (1980). *Behind closed doors: Violence in American families.* New York: Doubleday.

Stryker, J., Coates, T., De Carlo, P., Haynes-Sanstad, K., Shriver, M., & Makadon, H. J. (1995, April 12). *Journal of the American Medical Association.*

Sullivan, C. M. (1991, August). Battered women as active helpseekers. *Violence Update,* pp. 1, 8.

Sullivan C. M., Campbell, R., Angelique, H., Eby, K. K., & Davidson, W. S., II. (1994). An advocacy intervention program for women with abusive partners: Six-month follow-up. *American Journal of Community Psychology, 22,* 101-122.

Szinovacz, M. E. (1983). Using couple data as a methodological tool: The case of marital violence. *Journal of Marriage and the Family, 45,* 633-644.

Taves, A. (Ed.). (1989). *Religion and domestic violence in early New England.* Bloomington: Indiana University Press.

Tolman, R. M., & Bennett, L. W. (1990). A review of research on men who batter. *Journal of Interpersonal Violence, 5*(1), 87.

Tomes, H. (1995). Research and policy directions in violence: A developmental perspective. *Journal of Health Care for the Poor and Underserved, 6*(2), 146-151.

Torres, S. (1991). A comparison of wife abuse between two cultures: Perceptions, attitudes, nature, and extent. *Issues in Mental Health Nursing, 12,* 113-131.

University of Colorado. (1994). *Percentage of women murdered by their male intimate partners: Unpublished analysis of 1988-1991 FBI Uniform Crime Reports.* Center for the Study and Prevention of Violence, at the Institute for Behavioral Science, University of Colorado.

U.S. Bureau of the Census. (1990). *Census of population and housing* (Summary tape file 3 on CD-ROM technical documentation). Washington, DC: Author.

Volpp, L. (1994). (Mis)identifying culture: Asian women and the "cultural defense." *Harvard Women's Law Journal, 17,* 57.

White, E. C. (1994). *The black women's health book: Speaking for ourselves.* Seattle, WA: Seal Press.

Whitehurst, R. (1971). Violence potential in extramarital sexual responses. *Journal of Marriage and the Family, 11,* 688.

Williams, O., & Becker, R. L. (1994). Domestic partner abuse treatment programs and cultural competence: The results of a national survey. *Violence and Victims, 9*(3), 287-296.

Wilson, M., Johnson, H., & Daly, M. (1993). Lethal and nonlethal violence against wives. *Canadian Journal of Criminology, 37*(3), 331-362.

World Bank Report. (1993). *The world development report.* New York: Oxford University Press.

Index

About the Authors

Doris Williams Campbell, PhD, ARNP, is Director of Diversity Initiatives for the University of South Florida Health Sciences Center, Tampa, FL, and Professor in the Colleges of Nursing and Public Health. She is a member of the Governor's Task Force on Domestic Violence, State of Florida and the State of Florida Clemency Panel for Domestic Violence Review. Her research interest is violence against women with a special focus of research and practice issues related to violence and abuse in the lives of African American women and abuse during pregnancy. Recent publications include Campbell, J. C. & Campbell, D.W. (1996). Cultural competence in the care of abused women. *Journal of Nurse Midwifery,* 41, (6), 457-462, and Gary, F., Campbell, D., & Serlin, C. (1996). African American Women: Disparities in health care. *The Journal of the Florida Medical Association,* 83, (8), 489-493.

Jacquelyn Campbell received her BSN from Duke University, her MSN from Wright State University and her PhD from the University of Rochester. Her honors include membership in the American Academy of Nursing and a Kellogg National Leadership Fellowship. She is currently the Anna D. Wolf Endowed Professor and Director of the Doctoral Programs at Johns Hopkins University School of Nursing with a joint appointment in the School of Hygiene and Public Health. She is the Principal Investigator of five NIH, DOD, or CDC major funded research studies on battering and the author or co-author of more than 50 publications on the subject. These include the books *Nursing Care of Survivors of Family Violence, Sanctions and Sanctuary* and *Assessing Dangerousness* and a forthcoming text from Sage, *Beyond Diagnosis: Changing the Health Care Response to Abused Women and Their Children.* Dr. Campbell has worked with

177

wife abuse shelters and policy related committees on domestic violence for more than 15 years. She is currently on the Board of Directors of the House of Ruth, a shelter in Baltimore, the Family Violence Prevention Fund in San Francisco and the Institute of Medicine's Board on International Health.

Marissa Ghez, MA, is Associate Director of the Family Violence Prevention Fund and directs its national public education campaign, *There's No Excuse for Domestic Violence,* a collaborative effort with The Advertising Council that has already generated more than $40 million in donated time and space in 22,000 media outlets across the country. She has also developed many innovative communications initiatives designed to advance public recognition of domestic violence as a public health problem, including developing the concept and partners for a novel radio series following a soap-opera-like format targeting the African-American community, as well as creating the first national domestic violence presence on the World Wide Web. The initiative has won numerous awards, most recently a Clarion Award from Women in Communications, Inc. for best multi-media advertising campaign.

Ethel Klein is currently President of EDK Associates, a strategic research firm. She has designed strategic education campaigns for nonprofit organizations and foundations on issues of women's rights, environmental protection, voter registration, work and family policies, arms control, and tax reform. Previously, this longtime analyst of American politics was a professor of political science at Harvard University (1979-1984) and Columbia University (1984-1990). She is also the author of the groundbreaking *Gender Politics,* and she is credited with helping Richard Gephardt develop his populist style and message.

Beckie Masaki, MSW, is Co-Founder and Executive Director of the Asian Women's Shelter in San Francisco. She has worked in the field of domestic violence since 1983, first as a staff member at La Casa de las Madres battered women's shelter, then as one of the founders of the Asian Women's Shelter. She is chair of the San Francisco Domestic Violence Prevention Fund and advisory committee member for the National Domestic Violence Hotline. She has provided training on the local, state, national, and international levels, most recently in Japan for an international symposium on domestic violence.

Esta Soler is Founder and Executive Director of the San Francisco-based Family Violence Prevention Fund, a national organization working to develop innovative responses to the epidemic of domestic violence. She has served as consultant and adviser on domestic violence to many private and governmental organizations, including the National Institute of Justice, the U.S. Department of Health and Human Services, the Centers for Disease Control and Prevention, the Ford

Foundation, and the Milbank Memorial Fund. She has been appointed to serve on the Presidential Commission on Crime Control and Prevention and the National Advisory Council on Violence Against Women, and she has received numerous awards for her work on domestic violence and women's rights.

Sara Torres is Associate Professor and chair of the Department of Psychiatric, Community Health, and Adult Primary Care at the School of Nursing, University of Maryland at Baltimore. She has a long history of involvement in the struggle for the empowerment of Hispanic battered women. She is also involved in the recruitment, retention, and career mobility of Hispanics in the nursing field. Her major academic and research interests focus on the Hispanic community. She has been funded by the National Institutes of Health to conduct research on Hispanic battered women and published the first article in a refereed journal on this topic. She is a nationally recognized expert in this area and is frequently sought as a consultant.